me-changer! This incredibly powerful story will change your life. Anyone
any generation or background can use this book to fuel their dreams and
wer their future."

—Sarah Jakes Roberts, author, businesswoman, and media personality

.d Bach's advice is masterful. He takes the complicated and makes it
e—it's literally a three-step process to financial freedom. You can do this!"

—Jon Gordon, bestselling author of *The Energy Bus* and
The Power of Positive Leadership

Latte Factor will completely transform your relationship with money and
ness. I read seventy to a hundred books a year, and this one rocked me. It
tally flip your mind-set upside down and give you a 10X better operating
n for life."

—Benjamin P. Hardy, contributor to Inc.com

y single woman in America needs to read this book. David Bach is the
ate crusader for women's financial empowerment—and *The Latte Factor*
v your guide to the financial security and freedom you deserve."

—Dottie Herman, president and CEO of Douglas Elliman

nstant classic, *The Latte Factor* is the perfect gift for people of any age who
like to think about finances—and are poorer and unhappier because of it.
: one hour to read this book and reap positive returns for a lifetime!"

—Ken Blanchard, #1 bestselling coauthor of
The New One Minute Manager and *The Secret*

 and Mann's *The Latte Factor* will help you learn how to best identify
you value most, so you can spend, save, and invest to live a life aligned
our goals."

—Erin Lowry, author of *Broke Millennial Takes On Investing*

y college student across America and around the world needs to read this
 David's advice is so powerful because it is so easy to implement, and the
e shares is both heartfelt and inspirational."

—Dr. Jennifer Aaker, General Atlantic Professor at
Stanford Graduate School of Business

d Bach has never failed to amaze me with his genius for making the com-
vorld of finances approachable to everyone and his genuine caring about
g an impact in people's lives. *The Latte Factor* is a book for all time!"

—Louis Barajas, author of *The Latino Journey to Financial Greatness*

May 15, 2019

Carrie!
My Sister!!
May we always
share "a latte"
together!

I love you!
Janice

"Iconic financial expert David Bach has inspired tens of millions of lives with his Latte Factor method. You owe it to yourself to read *The Latte Factor* and share it with those who matter most to you. In less than an hour you'll learn truly how to become a financial grownup."

—Bobbi Rebell, CFP°, author of *How to Be a Financial Grownup*, host of the *Financial Grownup* podcast, and former Reuters business TV anchor

"A captivating story packed with aha moments. *The Latte Factor* will surprise and delight you—and it will transform the way you think about personal finances."

—Michael Hyatt, *New York Times* bestselling author of *Platform* and *Your Best Year Ever*

"Bach and Mann offer a master class in the fundamentals of personal finance and financial independence, wrapped in an engaging story of self-discovery. *The Latte Factor* is a gem!"

—Bob Roth, *New York Times* bestselling author of *Strength in Stillness*

"Bach and Mann have done a startlingly good job of illustrating life's deepest secret and most profound truth: that a genuinely rich life—a life of 'flat-out, un-bridled joy,' as the authors put it—is available to anyone in any circumstances. Highly recommended!"

—Sally Helgesen, coauthor of *How Women Rise* and author of *The Female Advantage*

"I LOVE this book! In one fun-filled hour, you will learn how a few small, simple changes can compound into a massive transformation in your financial future. *The Latte Factor* is destined to be a global sensation!"

—Darren Hardy, *New York Times* bestselling author of *The Compound Effect* and former publisher and editor of *SUCCESS* magazine

"A great read for millennials, and a helpful reminder that little life changes can have a big impact on your financial future."

—Jessica Moorhouse, founder of Millennial Money Meetup and host of *Mo' Money* podcast

"A game-changing little book, delivered with the wisdom, heart, and brilliant simplicity that have endeared David Bach to millions. Read, act now (it's easier than you think), and genuine financial freedom is yours for the taking!"

—Dan Sullivan, The Strategic Coach Inc.

"A wonderful, fun, engaging, inspiring book! You'll love the story so much you'll forget that you're actually learning life-changing lessons from a master in the field."

—Bob Burg, bestselling coauthor of *The Go-Giver*

The

LATTE
FACTOR®

*Why You Don't Have to
Be Rich to Live Rich*

DAVID BACH
and John David Mann

ATRIA BOOKS

New York London Toronto Sydney New Delhi

ATRIA
BOOKS

An Imprint of Simon & Schuster, Inc.
1230 Avenue of the Americas
New York, NY 10020

First Atria Books hardcover edition May 2019

ATRIA BOOKS and colophon are trademarks of Simon & Schuster, Inc.

The Latte Factor and *The Latte Factor Challenge* are
registered trademarks of David Bach and FinishRich Media LLC.

For information about special discounts for bulk purchases, please contact
Simon & Schuster Special Sales at 1-866-506-1949
or business@simonandschuster.com.

Interior design by Joy O'Meara

Manufactured in the United States of America

10 9 8 7 6 5 4 3 2 1

Library of Congress Cataloging-in-Publication Data

Names: Bach, David, author. | Mann, John David, author.
Title: The latte factor : why you don't have to be rich to live rich /
David Bach and John David Mann.
Description: New York, NY : Atria Books, [2019]
Identifiers: LCCN 2018058139 (print) | LCCN 2019000454 (ebook) |
ISBN 9781982120245 (eBook) | ISBN 9781982120238 (hardcover)
Subjects: LCSH: Finance, Personal. | Wealth.
Classification: LCC HG179 (ebook) | LCC HG179 .B236 2019 (print) |
DDC 332.024/01—dc23
LC record available at https://urldefense.proofpoint.com/v2/url?u=https-3A__lccn.loc.go
v_2018058139&d=DwIFAg&c=jGUuvAdBXp_VqQ6t0yah2g&r=06HB5XcKNe3kUU3
6TuOk0fMyO_eF5k6L7zVOIl7jYavLVBqUfi1IqLi0uMcjKSVc&m=6Z95_R
-cCvcvyrq58Dcl_sv0qwCDakaHgsrJajhaowk&s=G-OLZUTUzU9ntFOpe5BNx1fHQ
_rlCL_wrZHvG6IgbQU&e=

ISBN 978-1-9821-2023-8
ISBN 978-1-9821-2024-5 (ebook)

To Oprah Winfrey
—who allowed me the opportunity to share
the Latte Factor on your life-changing show
and reach tens of millions of people.

To Paulo Coelho
—your words, "David, you must write this book!"
pushed me to finally write *The Latte Factor*.

To Alatia Bradley Bach
—who listened to me talk about doing this book for a decade
and never doubted that I would.

I am beyond grateful to you all.

Contents

The
LATTE
FACTOR®

CHAPTER I

The Oculus

Boarding the L train to work Monday morning, as she did every day, Zoey took a sip of her double-shot latte and thought about the photograph.

She thought about it for the full forty minutes it took to travel west and then south, from Brooklyn to her last stop in Lower Manhattan, and she thought about it as she stood to exit the train along with a thousand other passengers.

What *was* it about that photograph?

The subway car doors opened and Zoey became a drop in the ocean of commuters as it poured through Fulton Center, the hub where nearly every subway line in Lower Manhattan converged. The wave carried her along through the gray-tiled passageway and out into the huge open space below the World Trade Center, where Zoey stopped, rooted in place, as people flowed around her. She glanced up at the cavernous ceiling. It looked like the ribs of an enormous bird cast in white steel, a phoenix risen from the ashes of 9/11.

She began moving again, feeling the hugeness of the place as she walked. Six hundred feet of pure white Italian marble. It was like being in a gigantic cathedral.

The Oculus. Gateway to one of the most famous memorials and tourist destinations in the world. Zoey passed through it every day—twice, in fact: once on the way to work and then again on the way home—yet she'd never really stopped to take it in.

She entered the white marble–lined West Concourse passageway, with its enormous LED wall display to her left, nearly a football field in length. Normally she ignored the constant rotation of advertisements and public service announcements, intent only on getting to the escalator. Today the image splashed across the big screen made Zoey stop in her tracks once more.

The picture showed a fishing boat, complete with crew and nets—very much like the boat in that photograph, the one she couldn't get out of her mind. Only, rather than rocking in the water at dockside, this boat sat stranded in the middle of a desert.

Strange, thought Zoey. Strange, and strangely unsettling.

As she watched, giant letters scrolled across the image, spelling out a message:

**If you don't know where you're going,
you might not like where you end up.**

Moments later the image dissolved, replaced by more ads. Zoey walked on.

Reaching the end of the passageway, she stepped onto the escalator, which carried her two stories up and into the sunlit glass atrium. She walked outside and turned back toward West Street, the sun in her eyes, to face the building where she worked. One World Trade Center, the tallest building in the Western Hemisphere. This was her daily routine. She loved standing in this spot, tipping her head way back and looking straight up, trying to see the top of the enormous tower as it stretched toward the sky.

Today, though, her mind was elsewhere.

If you don't know where you're going, you might not like where you end up.

It was an ad for something—insurance company, car company, travel app, she couldn't quite remember what. Hadn't Jessica had something to do with that slogan? It seemed to her that this was one of Jess's accounts, whatever it was they were advertising. Yet this morning somehow it felt like a personal message directed right at Zoey. And it gnawed at her.

Just like that photograph. The one she couldn't get out of her mind.

She suddenly remembered the latte in her left hand and took a sip. It had gone cold.

Normally she would now cross the street, enter the building, and take the elevator up to her office on the thirty-third floor. Today she diverted from her usual path. After crossing over West Street, she took a sharp right, heading away from One World Trade, and walked toward the reflecting pools, the two enormous square fountains built on the precise footprints of the original Twin Towers, bordered by short black marble walls with an endless stretch of names carved into their top surfaces.

The 9/11 Memorial.

She stopped at the north pool and looked down at the surging water below. Felt the surface of the marble and read the first dozen names. There were so many of them. Thousands of people had died here, in those dark days of September 2001. Zoey had been in grade school then. She glanced over at the great ribbed wings of the Oculus jutting up among the skyscrapers a block away.

Why did everything look so different to her today?

If you don't know where you're going, you might not like where you end up.

Where exactly was it that Zoey was going? Where exactly did she expect to end up?

Had she ever really thought about that before?

A man stopped for a split second to glare at the watch on his wrist, then hurried on. Zoey stirred. She was going to be late for work.

She started to turn away to head back toward One World Trade Center—but something held her in place. Instead, she stepped over to one of the nearby concrete benches and sat down, cold latte in hand, as the stream of tourists, commuters, and locals flowed past. She spoke softly, to no one but herself:

"What am I doing with my life?"

CHAPTER 2

The Photograph

Zoey's day hit with full force the moment she stepped out of the elevator on the thirty-third floor, as it did every Monday morning. The spring issue deadline was coming up on Friday, and everyone in the office was in full production mode. A flood of articles, bios, and photo captions all clamored for Zoey's attention—mountain biking in Ecuador, wine tasting in the Balkans, photo-essays with famous travelers' names in the bylines—and it was her job to shape and polish their scribbles into perfect sparkling prose.

Zoey worked at a large publishing company with offices in One World Trade Center. The Freedom Tower, they called it. Which always seemed a little ironic to Zoey, because as much as she liked the rush of work, she would hardly describe the time she spent within those walls as *free*. She was grateful for the position, but she worked punishing hours and the pay was not nearly as glamorous as their readers probably would have guessed.

And talk about irony: here she was, twenty-seven years old, an associate editor for a world-famous travel magazine—and she'd never been outside the US. Or west of the Mississippi, for that matter. She didn't even have a passport.

A travel editor who never traveled.

She plopped down her laptop, flipped it open, logged on to the staff network, and got to work, her fingers flying over the keyboard.

Zoey thrived on the chaos of it. The insane deadlines, the last-minute content changes, the challenge of taking a piece of decent-to-mediocre writing and shaping it into a thing of quality. She pushed away that vague sense of unease she'd had and hunched over her keyboard as she slipped into the rhythm of the place.

"Are we hungry yet?"

Zoey straightened in her chair and rotated her neck to get out the kinks. Was it really already past one o'clock? She turned to find her boss watching her from behind the half partition that defined Zoey's workstation.

"Even virtual world travelers have to eat sometime," her boss added.

Barbara was not as hip or fashion forward as most of the magazine staff. In the upscale environment of Lower Manhattan, it sometimes seemed to Zoey that Barbara was a visitor from a small town who had never quite adapted to her new environment. (More or less the opposite of Jessica, in other words.) But she was exceptionally smart and had a natural empathy and keen sense of what was going on under the surface of things. Zoey supposed that was what made her such a great editorial director.

When Zoey first started there six years earlier, it was Barbara who made the hire, and the two had clicked immediately. Barbara had high expectations and exacting standards. She was a "tough" boss, in that sense—but she didn't push people. It was more like she *pulled*. It wasn't that you were afraid of her; it was that you didn't want to disappoint her.

And Zoey never did. She was a ferocious editor, and very good at her job.

"Famished," said Zoey. She put her laptop to sleep and followed Barbara to the elevator to head upstairs for lunch.

The company cafeteria overlooked downtown Manhattan and the Hudson, with a good view of the Statue of Liberty. With its open spaces and austere decor, the café looked like any high-end Manhattan lunch spot. When Zoey first started working there, she'd had to get used to the occasional celebrity sightings.

Barbara had brought her simple lacquer lunch box, which she unpacked with deliberate care while Zoey went through the lunch line and selected a complicated chicken salad with quinoa, Marcona almonds, and organic baby greens. As she began picking at her salad, she made a stab at chatting about the article she was currently working on, but small talk was not her forte and she trailed off after two sentences.

In the brief silence that followed, Barbara worked on her sandwich and regarded Zoey.

"So," she finally said. "You seem . . . off your game today. Everything okay?"

There was that Barbara perceptiveness for you. Zoey had tried to forget all about that strange mood that had taken her over this morning, but her boss had sensed it anyway. She took a quiet breath and let it out. She wasn't sure quite where to start, because she didn't fully understand it herself.

"You'll think this is weird," Zoey began.

Barbara took another bite of her sandwich and nodded, as if to say, *Go on.*

"On the way to the train, in the morning, there's this coffee shop where I always stop, right in Williamsburg." As she began describing where the place was located, Barbara nodded again.

"Helena's Coffee."

"You know it?"

Barbara looked at Zoey over her sandwich and said: "And?"

"Okay," Zoey began. "So there's this framed photograph hanging on the back wall. I mean, there are a lot of framed photographs there, the place is covered with them. But there's this one in particular."

You could just see it from the order line up front, where Zoey would wait for her latte and breakfast muffin. Helena's was the kind of place where the snack items were always ultra-fresh, the coffee was reliably delicious, and the prints on the walls were stunning.

She described the photograph, then went silent as she worked on her salad.

"And?" added Barbara after a moment.

"And, I don't know. I've just been thinking about it, is all. I'm not sure why."

Zoey carved clean sentences for a living, but she wasn't doing a very good job of it right now.

"And you want it."

Zoey sighed. Of course she wanted it.

It was a simple enough scene: a little seaside village at dawn, the first rays of sunlight casting an amber-golden glow that sparkled like jewels, and, in the foreground, a fishing boat crew readying their vessel to head out to sea. Golden Hour, they called it, that time just after sunrise when the light reddened and became almost liquid. To Zoey there was something magical about it, a hushed moment bursting with unseen energy, held suspended for all time on a silken thread.

The photo print was good-sized, probably four feet wide by three feet high. Even so, she'd never seen much detail, because she'd never spent enough time in the place to go over and really study it. Every morning she would leave her apartment (usually a little late), rush to the coffee shop to pick up her double-shot latte and muffin, then fast-walk to the stop just in time for the L train to whisk her off to Manhattan. She barely had time for a glance around as she paid for her order. Yet, even in those brief glimpses, there was something about that photograph that always called to her. This morning, she'd paused a half minute longer to take it in, moved a step or two closer. It was just one little moment, really—but it had been enough to fix the picture vividly in her mind.

She knew just the spot on her living room wall where she would hang it. Although maybe "living room" was a stretch; more like her living room/dining room/home office. Zoey lived with a roommate in a cramped little apartment, and it wasn't much to look at. That big sunlit oceanside scene would transform the place.

"It's not that I want to *own* it, necessarily. It's just . . ." Just what? The photograph had stirred up feelings in Zoey that she couldn't quite describe, let alone explain. "I don't know." She shook her head, as if dismissing the thought. "I don't even know that it's for sale. And anyway, even if it is—"

And Barbara spoke the next four words together with her, the two in perfect unison:

"*I can't afford it.*"

In the song that was Zoey's life, that was the chorus. The verses might be inspiring, adventurous, or contemplative—*I'd love to go back to school, tour the American Southwest, travel Europe, have a place with an actual bedroom where I could write and do some yoga*—but they always came back around to the same refrain: *But I can't afford it.*

And she truly couldn't. Brooklyn wasn't as expensive as living in Manhattan, but it was still pricey. And then there were her student loans, which sat on her like a hundred-pound backpack filled with bricks. It was a good thing she lived in the city, where she didn't need a car, because if she had one, it probably would have been repossessed by now. Car? Ha! The way things were going, her *bicycle* would probably be repossessed by summertime.

Zoey was skilled with words and had a good visual sense. But numbers? Not her thing. And she was terrible with money, always had been. She'd tried to organize herself with a budget, as her mother had urged her to do—"budget" being probably Zoey's least favorite word in the English language. That, of course, had been a dismal failure. At work she was fiercely structured and productive, but when it came to her own money, she had zero discipline. That was just the way things were. Here it was, March, and she was still buried in card charges she'd run up buying the previous year's round of Christmas presents for family and friends. Probably those from the year before that, too, if she took the time to sort through the statements. Charges on top of charges on top of charges.

Yes, Zoey liked her job, and she was good at it; but she had to admit, she was barely making ends meet. In fact, the ends weren't really *meeting* at all—more like catching glimpses of each other from across the room every now and then. Zoey thought she would qualify as poster child for the phrase "living paycheck to paycheck."

Whatever that photo print actually cost—$500? $800? $1,000?, if it was for sale at all—it was certain to be a chunk of cash she did *not* have just lying around waiting to be spent on a whim.

———

Barbara's voice cut into her thoughts: "You should talk to Henry."

"Henry?"

"The older guy you see in there, in the mornings, making the coffee? That's Henry."

It took Zoey a moment to register what Barbara was talking about. "You mean, at the coffee shop? You know the barista at Helena's?"

Barbara stood up, closing her empty lunch box as she did. "Known him for years. You should go in and talk to him. He sees things . . ." She paused. "He sees things *differently*."

"Talk to the barista?" said Zoey. "And say . . . ?"

Barbara gave Zoey her trademark blank expression, a face that saw everything and gave nothing away. "Just talk to him. Tell him you love the print. See what he says."

Zoey frowned.

"Trust me," said Barbara. "He's resourceful."

"And he'll help me do what, exactly? Pick the right lottery ticket?"

Barbara shrugged. "Probably not that. But you said it yourself: you can't afford it. And that bothers you. Am I right?"

Zoey said nothing. Of course she was right. She was Barbara.

"Well, then," said Barbara. "*Do* something about it. Talk to Henry."

Heading back to her desk, Zoey felt a twinge of guilt. She hadn't told Barbara what was *really* nagging at her. And it wasn't just the photograph. It was the other thing.

The agency job.

Two Fridays ago, over drinks, her old college roommate Jessica told her about a position opening up at the media agency uptown where Jess worked. "You're a hard worker, Zoe," she'd said. "You're smart, you're a fantastic writer, and people love you. You'd be perfect."

So Zoey had slipped uptown one day the week before and interviewed for the job. That same night Jessica called and told her that, from what she'd heard, Zoey was the odds-on favorite. "There were a ton of candidates, Zoe—but you hit it out of the park." Sure enough, this past Friday the agency called to give her the news: she was officially their first choice. If Zoey wanted the job, it was hers for the taking—and at considerably higher pay than at her current post. She knew it would mean higher stress and a brutal schedule, which didn't thrill her at all. But that agency salary would really turn things around for her.

She'd talked with Mom about it again over the weekend. Her mother wasn't so sure about the idea. "Oh, Zee," Mom had said, "be happy with what you have! Besides, sweetheart, money won't make you happy."

Money won't make you happy. How many times had Zoey heard that growing up?

Her father had gotten on the phone, too, which was unusual. "Think about this, Zoey," he'd said. Zoey knew what that meant: *I don't want to come right out and say you should take the job . . . but yeah, maybe you should take the job.*

Her dad had made decent money as a general contractor, until his health forced him to ride a desk at some building supply company. It was far less pay (and, she suspected, far less fun), but they were managing. Although Mom sounded even more worn-out than usual lately. *Be happy with what you have.* Her parents were not *unhappy*, she was sure of that, but could she describe them as truly *happy*?

And what about Zoey herself?

She thought again of that strange image from the Oculus that morning, of the boat beached in the middle of the desert. *If you don't know where you're going . . .*

The people at the agency uptown had given Zoey a week to work out the details of leaving her current job and make her decision official. Which meant that if Zoey wanted the job, she needed to give them a firm commitment by this Friday. After which she and Jessica would celebrate the deal together at their usual Friday meet-for-drinks-after-work date.

The only other alternative Zoey could see was to keep struggling on her current salary and hope for another promotion. And meanwhile, maybe, take on some additional freelance writing or editing, jammed somehow—along with the extra load of work she typically brought home from her day job—into the evenings and weekends. An idea that *definitely* did not thrill her.

But what other option did she have?

CHAPTER 3

You're Richer Than You Think

"*Do* something," Barbara had said. The next morning Zoey did something. She got ready for work and left her apartment fifteen minutes early. She didn't see the point in talking to the barista, as Barbara had urged, but at least she could spend a little time inside Helena's Coffee and get a closer look at that photo print.

She put in her order, stood in line, then took her double-shot latte and began strolling through the place, taking it all in. Exposed brick, vaulted ceiling (painted black so it all but disappeared), big pendant lamps with full-spectrum bulbs, and big, artfully lit photographs covering the walls, making the place feel like one of Brooklyn's trendy art galleries. Trendy, but old-school.

She walked all around the coffee shop perimeter, looking at the sequence of prints. Some were of breathtaking panoramas: snow-covered mountaintops, raging rivers caught in mid-splash, vast forest tracts. A few were in locations she thought she recognized from her work at the magazine. There was a shot of the Great Wall, another of a few young men working the family vineyard in the Italian Piedmont. A brilliantly colored flock of macaws in the Peruvian rainforest.

They were all amazing, but she kept walking—until she reached The Photograph.

This was the one. This one. She stood in place, some six feet back, gazing at it.

It was not a spectacular scene, really, at least not on the surface. A seaside village at dawn. A little fishing boat, just visible on the right, preparing for the day's catch. People trundling to and fro along the little harbor, going about their village business.

What was it exactly that drew her so?

She took a few steps closer, enough to read the tiny printed inscription posted just below the right-hand corner. Ah. So it did have a price tag: $1,200.

Zoey's heart sank. Pricey for a photo, but then, this was an exceptional piece, wasn't it. And, really, $1,200 was not all that much in the big scheme of things. It was less than a month's rent. Zoey *ought* to be able to afford it. But she couldn't remember the last time she'd seen that kind of money just sitting in her bank account, available to spend on whatever she wanted.

Oh, right, now she remembered when: that would be *never*.

She bent down and looked at the label again, to see where the shot was taken, but it didn't say. In fact, other than the price, the only information provided was the photograph's title, which consisted of a single word, in quotes:

"Yes"

Yes. It seemed like an odd title for a photo of a seaside village. *Yes* what? Although, now that she looked at it again, it certainly felt like a *Yes* to her. What *was* the location? Had to be one of the Greek islands. "Where are you?" she murmured. "Rhodes? Santorini?" No, that wasn't it. "Crete?"

"*Mykonos.*"

The voice was so close to her ear, it made Zoey jump, and she nearly spilled her latte.

"Sorry," the man said. "Didn't mean to sneak up on you. You were pretty focused there." He nodded at the photograph. "Caught your eye, that one?"

Zoey nodded. "It's beautiful. The light is amazing. Very *Yes*," she added, pointing at the label. The elderly man peered at the label, then nodded. She stuck out her hand. "I'm Zoey. Zoey Daniels."

The man shook her hand. His skin was dry and cool, like fine canvas. "Henry Haydn," he said. He pronounced it *hidin'*, as in "hide-and-seek." "Like the composer," he added. "Though not as famous."

"Henry," she said. Of course. She recognized him now: the barista. "Maybe more famous than you realize."

The man cocked his head, as if to say, *Oh?*

"My boss told me about you," Zoey explained. "Said I should come in and talk to you."

"Ah," he said. "About what?"

Zoey opened her mouth to answer, then closed it again, then grinned at him. "You know, I have no idea."

He smiled and nodded toward the photo. "Don't see a lot of people gravitate to this one," he said. "Mostly people are drawn to the more dramatic shots, you know? Mountains, canyons, river rapids, things like that."

Zoey could understand that. "This one, though," she said. "It just seems so . . . *alive*."

Henry nodded. "Personally, it's my favorite out of all of 'em."

Zoey stood and did a slow 360-degree turn, looking all around the place, then back at Henry. "Mine too."

He cocked his head again. "Well. It's not taken, you know."

Zoey laughed. "I wish! But I'm afraid I couldn't afford it."

Henry nodded at the latte in her hand. "If you can afford that latte," he said, and he tipped his head back toward the wall, "you can afford this photograph."

"Sorry?" she said. Had she heard him right? That made no sense at all.

"Perhaps," said Henry, "*you're richer than you think.*"

She gave a puzzled smile, thinking, *What an odd thing to say.* Still, she liked his energy. "That's a very nice thought," she said. "Really, though, I'm just looking." She leaned closer again, scouring the background for detail: the narrow cobblestoned streets, whitewashed houses, the royal-blue doors and shutters. "Mykonos . . . You think?"

Henry leaned in, too, then slowly nodded. "I do."

"It's *so* beautiful." Zoey sighed. "What I'd *really* love," she spoke softly, as if talking to herself, "is to *be* there, smell that salt spray, hear those seagulls. Take in the whole scene with my own eyes and ears."

She straightened up again with a self-conscious laugh, then spoke in her normal voice. "Anyway. *That's* totally out of the question."

"Totally - out of - the question," he repeated, speaking slowly, as if musing over the words. He cocked his head at her. "But that would depend on the question. No?"

Zoey wasn't sure what to say to that.

"You like photography," he said. "Tell me. Do you know the term 'oculus'?"

"By Fulton Center," she said. "I'm actually headed there right now."

"No, no," he said. "Not the structure. I mean, in photography."

Zoey frowned.

"Oculus," he repeated. "It means figuring out where you want to stand. Where you stand, and what you see from there, is the key to putting together the right picture. That's what creates the perspective you want. You know what I mean?"

Zoey nodded, although, to be honest, she was not at all sure she did.

"In photography," the barista continued, "the oculus is where you place the camera. It's Latin for eye. Only it's really *your e*... Because you see the picture first, you see, in your mind's eye your oculus."

"Okay," said Zoey. She had never looked into the meaning.

"Now, I'm saying *photography*," he added, "but you as easily say a story you're going to write. A trip you take. A meal you're preparing in your kitchen for fri... be over in an hour or two. The point is, you're stan... there are three things: you, your lens, and the you create?"

What had Barbara said? *He's resourceful.* was the word that came to mind. But swee... nitely old-school—like the coffee shop its...

Henry Haydn glanced back toward t... to make sure he wasn't needed there. the beanie and long beard behind th... called over, "No worries, Henry. W...

Henry looked back at Zoey ar... high-top table in the corner. "J...

Zoey smiled. "Why not?"

She followed him over to the little table, where they each took a tall stool. He picked up a well-worn Moleskine notebook that lay on the table, flipped open the cover, took a brushed steel drafting pencil from a jacket pocket, and began sketching, his hand flying over the page. A few seconds later he turned the notebook so she could see it.

A grave plot and tombstone with neat lettering on it.

ZOEY DANIELS

BORN ?? — DIED ??

"Let's say, this is the end of your life."

"Really," said Zoey dryly. "So sad, she died so young."

Henry chuckled. "Humor me. Let's say we're writing your epitaph. Call it, your *oculus*." He tapped the sketch with his pencil. "Here is where you're standing, looking back at this pic- ure you've composed: your life. So, what does that landscape ›ok like?"

Zoey's breath caught.

She hadn't been able to put it into words, but what he'd just was *exactly* what had been bothering her the last few days. t did the landscape of her life look like? She didn't know.

you don't know where you're going, you might not like where d up.

u see?" said Henry. "The picture happens first in your ›ye. *Before* you shoot. That picture is where everything lat picture is what guides it all. Your *oculus*."

; phone buzzed. She glanced down. A text from an ‹n at work early, wanting to know which set of copyedits ‹.

"You need to get to work," ventured Henry.

"I really do," said Zoey apologetically. "Thanks for the . . . for the chat." She wasn't sure what else to call it. Art lesson? Notes on perspective?

"Nice talking with you," said Henry as she got to her feet and headed for the door. "Come back anytime."

When Zoey arrived at the thirty-third floor, the office was already in peak production uproar. She had a three-minute tactical meeting with the eager intern, checked in with the art department, then plopped down her laptop and lost herself in the crush of work.

Still, she couldn't quite stop her brain from mulling over her cryptic chat with the eccentric barista at Helena's. How had Barbara put it? *He sees things differently.* "That's for sure," she murmured to herself. The more she thought about their conversation, the less sense it made.

Where you stand, and what you see from there, is the key to putting together the right picture. That's what creates the perspective you want. You know what I mean?

Honestly, not a clue.

Then there was that comment about her coffee. *If you can afford that latte, you can afford this photograph.* And then this:

Perhaps you're richer than you think.

What was *that* about?

Zoey did not sleep well that night.

The truth was she didn't really sleep well *any* night. Typically she would wake up somewhere between two and three in the morning and lie awake, unable to drift back off, worrying. Not about anything specific — just a general kind of worrying.

This night, though, was worse than usual. This night after waking up, she *did* drift off again, and the worry followed her into her dreams.

She was jogging on the treadmill at her gym. Suddenly the machine sped up a notch, even though she hadn't touched any of the controls. No problem: she picked up her pace. The machine abruptly sped up again. She started running to keep up with it. She tried frantically to press the DOWN button to slow the treadmill, but instead it picked up yet again, and again, going faster and faster. She was sprinting now, racing full out, her heart pounding out of her chest, but she couldn't keep up—

She awoke with a gasp, her T-shirt drenched in sweat. Slowly, she sat up in bed and felt in the dark for the glass of water on her nightstand as her eyes adjusted and her heart rate gradually downshifted, from terror, to an earnest *thump-thump-thump*, and finally to something approaching normal.

You didn't need a PhD in psychology to interpret *that* little drama. She was on a fifty-hour-a-week treadmill she couldn't control. Brooklyn to Manhattan in the a.m., Manhattan back to Brooklyn in the p.m. Money in, money out—usually more out than in. And a creeping sense that, through it all, she was running for her life, going nowhere fast.

Gazing at her apartment walls in the semidarkness, she felt, as always in those moments when she was really honest with herself, that some element was absent in her life, something important. Love? No, she was young; there was plenty of time for that. Friends? No, she had Jessica and others.

What was missing in her life, she thought, was the *living* part.

CHAPTER 4

Pay Yourself First

On Wednesday morning Zoey arrived at the coffee shop a few minutes earlier than the day before. She found Henry in the back standing before The Photograph, apparently lost in thought. In a reversal of their first encounter the day before, this time it was she who startled him. "'Scuse me," she said.

He jumped slightly. "Ah, Zoey!" he exclaimed. "I was just enjoying our favorite print."

"Sorry," she said, adding, in exactly the same words he'd used with her the day before: "Didn't mean to sneak up on you. You were pretty focused there." She grinned, and he gave a mild laugh.

"Good memory," he said.

She gazed at the harbor scene again, then turned back to him. "I was wondering . . ." She hesitated, trying to figure out how to put it. "Yesterday, when you said, if I could afford my coffee, I could afford that photograph? That I might be richer than I think?"

Henry nodded.

"What did you mean, exactly?"

He cocked his head and put one finger to his lips for a moment, then said, "Let me ask you this: For you to be able to afford to buy this print, what would have to change?"

"Frankly, I'd need a job that paid more than I make now."

"Ah," he said. Then: "Do you mind if I get personal?"

"How could I mind?" said Zoey. "I mean, you've already drawn my tombstone. If that's not personal, I don't know what is."

"Excellent point," said Henry with a smile. "Where do you work again? Down in Lower Manhattan, you said?"

She nodded. "One World Trade." She briefly described her job at the travel magazine.

"I'd imagine that would pay pretty decent money," said Henry.

"Decent," she agreed, "but not exactly staggering. And living in Brooklyn is expensive."

"Indeed. If I may ask, how long have you been in the workforce, more or less?"

"About six years."

"All right. Enough time for a bright young person to advance in her position. My guess is you're earning a bit more now than you were six years ago. True?"

"True," said Zoey.

Henry nodded again. "So, are you richer today than you were six years ago as a result?"

Zoey blinked. "Richer?" She spoke the word as if it were in a foreign language.

"Do you, for example, have more disposable cash to spend on whatever you want? A little nest egg tucked away?"

In fact, Zoey had gotten a good bump in pay two years earlier, when Barbara promoted her from assistant editor to associate editor. But it seemed as if the more she made, the more it cost her just to live. If anything, she was deeper in the red than ever.

"Richer," Zoey repeated. "No, I would have to say, I am not richer."

"Well, you're not alone. I read a fascinating survey the other day. It said half the people in this country could not put their hands on an extra $400 even in the event of an emergency. Seven out of ten describe themselves as 'living paycheck to paycheck,' and many even put their everyday living expenses on credit cards."

"Really." Zoey was not surprised to learn that so many people were in the same boat she was. After all, wasn't that why her travel magazine was so popular? People loved to thumb through pages of adventures they couldn't afford to have themselves.

"Here's where it really gets interesting," said Henry. "When asked why they didn't save more or make some sort of retirement plan, nearly all the survey respondents gave the same answer: 'Not enough income.'" He chuckled. "At least, that's what they all said. It's not true, of course. More income wouldn't help their situation at all."

Zoey felt her brain snap to attention. "Wait—what?" She must have misheard him. "More income wouldn't help? But . . . that's exactly what *would* help!"

Henry shook his head sadly. "Not really. Most people, when they have more income, just spend it on more stuff."

"That's—" *That's not true,* Zoey was about to say. *That's not what I do, anyway.*

But was *that* true?

"How often do you read," the barista continued, "about some movie star, pop star, or sports star whose career skyrockets and they're suddenly worth millions, and the next thing you know they're broke?" Zoey had in fact read a story exactly like that, just the week before. "How many lottery winners end up in debt? For these folks, *making* the money isn't the problem, you see. The problem is *keeping* it.

"The strange truth, Zoey, is that earning more money—even outrageous amounts of money—does not necessarily lead to wealth. Why not? Because most people, when they earn more, simply spend more. Earnings are like the tide, you see, and your spending is like a boat. When the tide rises, the boat rises with it."

He cast his eye around the coffee shop, then back at Zoey. "Do you still have a little time before you have to go catch your train?"

"I do," she replied. After all, wasn't that exactly why she'd started out early this morning? As she followed Henry back to the little high-top table, she considered the image he'd just described: *Earnings are like the tide, and your spending is like a boat.*

Until it capsizes, she thought. *Or ends up run aground in a desert.*

"Wealth, financial freedom?" said Henry as he reached the table and turned back to face her. "Not that complicated. It's a simple three-step process."

"Let me guess," said Zoey. "Write a Top-40 song, hit the lottery, and have a rich great-aunt who's accident-prone?"

Henry laughed as he sat up on his stool. Zoey took the seat she'd had the day before.

"I call them the Three Secrets to Financial Freedom," said Henry. "Although that's perhaps a bit grandiose, because they're the kind of secrets that lie hidden in plain view. Everyone *thinks* they know about them, but hardly anyone *does* them.

"Let me tell you how the first secret works."

"All ears," said Zoey. *Eccentric, but insightful.* For the first time, she wondered what Henry's story was—where he came from, and how he had ended up working at a little coffee shop in Brooklyn.

"If I may ask," Henry was saying, "how many hours did you work last week?"

"Forty, more or less." It was really more like fifty, but close enough.

"All right. Now, how many of those hours did you work *for yourself?*"

Zoey started to reply but stopped before getting a word out. *All of them? None of them?* "I'm . . . I'm not clear on what you mean. Worked for myself, how?"

"Worked for yourself, as in, the money you earned went to *you.* To building your life. To investing in Zoey."

"Okay." She paused, then said, "I'm not really sure how to answer that."

"Well, let's look at it." He opened his well-worn Moleskine to a fresh page, took out his brushed steel drafting pencil, and began sketching as he talked.

"Let's say you start work at nine. Typically the pay you earn from nine to eleven thirty comes right off the top and goes straight to taxes."

He drew a clockface, blocking off the space from nine to eleven thirty and filling it with a bag of money and a tall, bearded Uncle Sam.

"Wow," murmured Zoey. "I never thought of it that way."

Henry nodded. "Kind of makes you want to come to work after lunch." He chuckled. "Then, from eleven thirty to two, you're paying your . . ." He glanced up at her. "Mortgage? Rent?"

"Rent," said Zoey. She was struck by how he sketched—a few strokes, sure and rapid, and he was done. The illustration seemed to spring complete from the tip of the pencil, as if it had been waiting in there to pop out.

"All right. Rent and utilities. From two to three typically goes to transportation costs. And from three to five, it's everything else: health care, entertainment, debt, credit cards . . ."

"Student loans," added Zoey.

"Ah, yes," he said. "Student loans. Vicious things. And of course groceries—"

"Eating out, mostly," put in Zoey.

"Ah," he said again. He nodded at the latte in her hand. "And the coffee."

"Yes," she said. "Let's not forget the coffee." They both smiled.

"Somewhere in there," he said, "you try to scrape off a few minutes' worth to save. Except most people don't. So, at the end of the day, there's nothing left to buy your photo print."

Despite how dismal that all sounded, Zoey couldn't help feeling a slight electric thrill ripple through her at those last few words. *Your photo print.* She nodded, curious to see just where this was all leading.

"All right, so I said three secrets, right? Here's secret number one."

He turned to a fresh blank page and wrote quickly in long, sweeping strokes:

1) *Pay Yourself First.*

"Pay yourself first," repeated Zoey, nodding to herself. "Sure."

"You've heard that before?" said Henry.

"I don't remember where exactly, but yes, it's a familiar concept."

"Excellent," said Henry. "Do you know what it means?"

Zoey was about to say *Of course*, but instead she paused, then said cautiously, "I . . . *think* I know what it means."

Henry smiled and raised his eyebrows. *Yes?*

"Well," said Zoey, "when I get paid, the first person I should spend money on is me." She looked at Henry. "No?"

Henry smiled again. "Close. That's what most people think it means: when you make money, you should treat yourself first. Buy yourself something nice, something you want."

"But that's not it?" said Zoey.

"Not exactly," said Henry. "What 'pay yourself first' means is that the first person who gets paid is you—and you *keep* that money. In other words: *you pay yourself the first hour of each day's income.*"

He turned to another fresh page in his notebook and began making a second sketch:

"When you go to work, you trade your time for money. Why would you work all day, every day," he said as he sketched, "and *not* keep at least an hour of that income for yourself? Yet here's how most people operate: When they're paid, the first thing they do, after the government takes its slice, is pay their bills and buy stuff. If there's anything left over—and that's a big if—*then* they save something to keep for themselves. Maybe. In other words, they pay *everyone else* first, and themselves last. If at all.

"That's why so many people work eight, nine, ten hours a day, week after week, month after month, for decades, an average of 90,000 *hours* over a lifetime—*ninety thousand!*—and at the end of the ride they get off and discover that they have nothing to show for it. That they've just spent their whole lives building someone else's wealth, but not their own."

Zoey was silent for a moment. Was that what her parents had done?

"Wow," she said.

"Wow, indeed," Henry agreed.

After another brief silence, Zoey said, "So, how is it *supposed* to work?"

Henry regarded her thoughtfully, then said, "When you were a kid, did you ever save your quarters in a jar? To save up for something you wanted to buy?"

In fact, Zoey had done exactly that—not as a kid but as an eighteen-year-old, freshly arrived in New York City to start college. All that summer she'd saved every dollar bill she could scrounge, and after three months she'd bought a bicycle so she could fully explore her new neighborhood. Which had amazed her, because she was normally terrible with money. She'd tried it other times, too, putting ten-dollar bills or even twenty-dollar bills in a jar on her kitchen counter for this purpose or that, but had never reached her goal. Something always came up, and she ended up raiding the jar. She still had that bike, though.

"Well, it's the same thing here," Henry said. "Only instead of putting quarters in a jar, you put your dollars into a 'pay yourself first' account. A retirement account, technically speaking."

"Like a 401 whatever," she said.

"Exactly," said Henry. "A 401(k)."

Zoey's company had a 401(k) plan; she remembered being told about it when she started working there. She'd gotten mailings and emails about it and kept meaning to sit down and go through them.

"The idea behind a 401(k) is simple," said Henry. "Every time you earn a paycheck, you set aside a portion of it—say, 10 percent—first, *before* it's taxed. Which totally changes how it compounds."

"How it compounds," she repeated. Zoey was fluent when it came to sentences and paragraphs, but math: again, not her thing.

Noting her expression, Henry said, "Here, let me demonstrate." He reached into his pocket for his wallet, took out a five-dollar bill, and placed it on the table between them.

"Let's say you took five dollars a day and put it in a jar. How much would you have after a week?"

"Five dollars a day, for a week?" said Zoey. That was easy. "Thirty-five dollars."

Henry nodded. "Which comes to about $150 per month. Now, let's say you put that daily five dollars into a pretax account where it earned, say, 10 percent interest per year. Do you know what you'd have at the end of the first year?"

Zoey thought about that. Twelve times $150. "I don't know, a little more than 1,500?"

Henry nodded. "One thousand eight hundred and eighty-five,

to be exact, with the interest included. Now, let's see what happens to that when you let the power of compound interest take over."

He slipped a small calculator out of his jacket pocket and began tapping away at it as he jotted down numbers. *Who still uses pocket calculators?* thought Zoey, smiling to herself. Her barista was *definitely* old-school.

He paused and looked up at Zoey. "Still saving five dollars a day, where do you think that would go after, say, forty years?"

"I don't know, maybe . . ." Zoey didn't see how it could be much more than $50,000, but, just to be safe, she doubled that amount. "A hundred thousand?"

Henry smiled. "Actually, almost ten times that amount." He turned the little notebook around so Zoey could read what he'd jotted down:

If you saved $5 a day and earned 10% annual interest, you'd wind up with:		
1 year	=	$1,885
2 years	=	$3,967
5 years	=	$11,616
10 years	=	$30,727
15 years	=	$62,171
30 years	=	$339,073
40 years	=	$948,611

Zoey stared at the numbers. "But . . . ," she stammered. "But that's nearly a million dollars!"

"It is," Henry agreed. He slipped another bill out of his pocket, this one a ten, and placed it on top of the five.

"Now let's say we raised the stakes and paid ourselves *ten* dollars a day, deposited into our pretax account. Let's see where *that* goes after forty years:

If you saved $10 a day and earned 10% annual interest, you'd wind up with:		
1 year	=	$3,770
2 years	=	$7,934
5 years	=	$23,231
10 years	=	$61,453
15 years	=	$124,341
30 years	=	$678,146
40 years	=	$1,897,224

Zoey's eyes widened as she scanned down the last few rows of numbers and saw the total at the bottom. "Whoa!" she said. "How . . . how did you *do* that?"

Henry chuckled. "*I* didn't do it, Zoey. Mother nature did it. That's the way nature works. It's how bacteria multiply. How rumors spread. How wealth is built. Some say it's the most powerful force in the universe. *The miracle of compound interest.*"

Zoey stared at his little chart. How was that possible?

"Just ten dollars a day . . . !" she murmured.

"Just ten dollars a day," Henry agreed. "But ten dollars a day can change your life. Because, make no mistake about it, Zoey: the action itself may seem small, even insignificant—the quarter in the jar, the ten dollars a day—but the decision to *do* it?" He smiled. "Might be the most important decision you'll ever make."

Zoey heard Barbara's voice in her head, saying, *Well, then.* Do *something about it.*

"Now, let me give you another example," said Henry. "One that's more to the point. How old are you now?" Before she could reply, he added, "I know a gentleman never asks, but this is for the sake of science. And your secret's safe with me."

"Well, if it's for science, then," Zoey deadpanned. "Twenty-seven."

"Perfect," said Henry. "So, let's just say you earn $1,000 a week—even I am discreet enough not to ask you how much you *actually* earn." Zoey laughed. In fact, that was pretty close to her actual gross pay. "That would be $200 a day," Henry continued. "Here's a good rule of thumb: *Keep your first hour's worth of each day's pay.* An hour a day, in other words, of paying yourself first.

"Most people don't even come close. The average American saves less than 4 percent of what they earn. In other words, most of us work barely twenty minutes for ourselves. And one in five saves nothing at all—that is, they pay themselves *zero.*"

"Ouch," murmured Zoey. That was her, all right. Total savings: nothing at all.

"Assuming you work an eight-hour day," Henry continued, "let's say we set aside the first hour of each day's pay for Zoey *to pay Zoey.* That would be"—he cocked his head as he did the calculation—"$25 a day, or $125 per week. Times fifty-two weeks, that comes out to $6,500 over the course of a year—nearly $6,800, when you add in the interest."

He started writing out another chart, tapping on his tiny calculator intermittently as he went.

Zoey felt her pulse quicken as she watched the numbers unfold from Henry's pencil.

If you saved $125 a week (or $25 per workday) and earned 10% annual interest, you'd wind up with:

1 year	=	$6,798
2 years	=	$14,308
5 years	=	$41,893
10 years	=	$110,821
15 years	=	$224,228
30 years	=	$1,222,924
40 years	=	$3,421,327

When he finished, he quietly set the pencil down and sat back on his stool, waiting.

Zoey sat stunned, staring at the numbers. *Over three million dollars. From one hour a day.*

Henry glanced at his wristwatch. "It's getting on," he said quietly. "You probably need to run."

With a start, Zoey looked at her phone and leapt to her feet. "Omigosh, I really do," she said.

"Here," said Henry, slipping off his stool. "I'll walk you to the door."

As they headed toward the front, Zoey said, "It seems so . . . I don't know. Too simple."

"It *is* simple," Henry replied. "That's why it works. It's usually the simplest ideas that change people's lives, not the complicated ones."

"Like your ten dollars a day," she said.

He nodded toward the latte in her hand and smiled again. "Like your coffee drink. Your *latte factor.*"

"Right," she said as they reached the front door. "My latte

factor." She had not the slightest idea what *that* was supposed to mean. "Well, thank you," she said. "That was most . . . educational." She reached out to shake his hand.

"Uh-huh," he said, reading the doubt in her face. He held on to her hand for an extra moment and peered at her. "Zoey," he said softly, "forget the numbers for the moment. What matters is what's *behind* the numbers. When you pay yourself first, what you're really doing is *putting yourself first.*"

Zoey frowned. She couldn't help it: she heard her mother's voice in her head saying, *Put others first, Zoey, always put others first.*

Henry gave a small nod. "I know: kind of goes against everything you've been taught, right? Nice people don't put themselves first. Good people think of *others* first. That what you were thinking?"

"Something like that," Zoey admitted.

He nodded. "And of course that's all quite true. A focus on service to others is the defining trait that makes us civilized human beings. But life is paradox, and sometimes the only way you *can* serve others is to put *yourself* first. You know what I mean by that?"

"To be honest," said Zoey, "I don't."

"You know that speech they always give on airplanes, when you're about to take off? About how, in the event there's a problem, you should put on your own oxygen mask first and *then* take care of the children? It sounds backwards. You'd think they'd tell you to take care of the kids first, right? But no. Because if you pass out, you're not going to be any good to *anyone.* You see?"

"I . . . think so," said Zoey.

Still holding her hand, Henry placed his other hand on top of hers. "Here's what I believe, Zoey. I believe that each one of us was put here on this earth, in this life, to do something, something special. Something no one else can do. And most of us aren't doing it—because we're too busy paying everyone else first."

————

Riding the L train to work, Zoey thought about what Henry had said. *I believe each one of us was put here to do something special. And most of us aren't doing it.*

Did she believe that?

And if she did, then what was Zoey put here to do?

CHAPTER 5

Doubts

Zoey drifted through work that day, editing on autopilot as she re-played snippets of her conversation with Henry. Finally, she took out her phone and began scrolling. On her ride into the city she had jotted down a few notes, and now she retyped them into her laptop, sorting and sequencing as she went.

This was what Zoey did. As an editor, she had developed the habit of sifting through the threads and fragments of narratives, like an archaeologist with a collection of unearthed bones, looking to see how it all fit together. Spelling, grammar, punctuation—all that could wait till later. What she looked for first was the big picture. What was the writer *saying*?

She looked at her notes.

Most people, when they earn more, simply spend more.
Everyone *thinks* they know about it, but hardly anyone *does* it.
Pay yourself first.
Some say it's the most powerful force in the universe.

Ten dollars a day can change your life.

Keep your first hour's worth of each day's pay.

And then there was that comment from the day before, the one that sounded like it came from a financial Zen master:

If you can afford that latte, you can afford this photograph.

She still had no idea what he meant by *that* one. Or by her "latte factor."

Her *latte factor?*

Walking home from the L train at the end of the day, she stopped in again at Helena's Coffee to see if she could get a moment with Henry, to ask him about that. But he was gone. He'd left at three that afternoon, the young guy behind the counter told her.

"Of course," said Zoey. After all, he'd been there at seven in the morning. "I guess his shift is long over."

"His shift?" The kid laughed. "Henry doesn't do shifts."

Doesn't do shifts? "So, when does he typically leave?" Zoey asked.

"Whenever he wants," said the kid, and he shrugged. "Usually around three, but could be later. Or earlier."

Whenever he wants? What kind of job was *that?*

She was still turning it all over in her mind when she unlocked the front door to her building, stepped into the vestibule, pushed the intercom button labeled JEFFREY GARBER, and announced, "Pizza in fifteen!"

Zoey's upstairs neighbor Jeffrey worked as a freelance developer of social media apps. He also did some tech support to pay the bills: search engine optimization, Facebook advertising, things like that. Social media apps, though, that was where he planned to strike it rich. He'd offered to cut Zoey in on several deals over the years, each one of which he was positive was going to be the next Instagram. Zoey had consistently declined.

So far, none of them had been the next Instagram.

Jeffrey was a nice enough guy, and she liked him, but she found she could take only so much of his cynical outlook. He had what seemed to Zoey a knee-jerk hostile reaction to "rich people," no matter who they were, and was especially suspicious of large, successful corporations. Like the one where she worked, for instance. (Although she had to wonder: If one of his apps struck market gold, wouldn't he *become* one of those big successful corporations?) Still, they were good friends, and they'd developed a routine of sharing dinner once a week, alternating who did the buying.

Tonight was Zoey's night. A large classic pizza with everything on it, from Luigi's. The best in Brooklyn: only a phone call away. (And no dirty dishes!)

This was one trait—one of the few, honestly—that Zoey and Jeffrey had in common. Jeffrey didn't cook. Neither did Zoey, other than toasted bagels and the occasional overdone omelet. Her mom had never cared much about cooking, and Zoey's family had put a good deal more mileage on the freezer and microwave than on the fridge or stove. Zoey's grandmother baked; her mother had rebelled. "Bake? I can't even make frosting!" she would say.

As they ate, Zoey told Jeffrey about her conversation with the eccentric barista.

There was something about Henry that made Zoey feel good being around him, something almost magnetic. Like charisma, but that wasn't quite it. She couldn't put her finger on it, much as she couldn't put her finger on what it was about that photograph that drew her so strongly.

Jeffrey listened to her narrative of the day's events without a word.

When she finished her share of the pizza, she wiped off her fingers and pulled out her laptop. At work that day, she'd taken the time to reproduce the chart Henry had drawn for her, with her theoretical $25 daily savings adding up to nearly $6,800 in the first year, and then that astronomical figure at the end of forty years.

She brought up the chart on her screen and showed it to Jeffrey.

"And look at this," she said. "After forty years, when I'm sixty-seven and eligible for full retirement? It's over *three million dollars*, Jeffrey!"

Her friend made an elaborate show of wiping off each finger, then sat back, licking them clean, and looked at her.

"Seriously?" he said. "Zoey, give me a break. Ten percent? How? Where are you gonna earn 10 percent? Interest rates like that are a relic of the past.

"Besides, the whole system is rigged, Zoe, you know that. The more you try to save, the more the government takes."

What had Henry said about setting aside a portion of your paycheck *before* it was taxed? Zoey either hadn't retained it or hadn't fully understood it in the first place.

"And then there's *inflation*. You know how much a million bucks will be worth in forty years? Ha. You'll be lucky to afford a slot in an old folks' home. And 401(k)s—they load those things up with so many rules and regs and restrictions, and it's all stacked against you. Anyway," he added, "who knows how long you'll be at that job? And when you leave, what happens to your retirement plan then?

"And, no offense, Zoe, but how exactly would *he* know? The guy's, what, in his sixties? Seventies? And he's still working as a barista?"

Zoey didn't have an answer for that.

After Jeffrey thanked her for the pizza and tromped back up the stairs to his apartment, Zoey spent the next forty-five minutes washing her hair, cleaning out her already mostly empty fridge, and scrubbing her rarely used stove top. It wasn't until she stopped and collapsed into her overstuffed TV chair that it occurred to her what the frenzy of cleaning was all about.

She was trying to scrub away the echoes of her friend's skeptical comments.

She had been excited about that chart of Henry's she'd managed to complete, and intrigued—even inspired—by his whole "everyone was put here for a reason" speech. She had to admit, the things he'd said had sparked a glint of pure bright *hope* somewhere inside her.

Jeffrey had shot all that down.

Interest rates like that are a relic of the past.

She picked up her phone, scrolled through her Favorites, and thumbed "Mom." After four or five rings, the line picked up.

"Hey, Mom."

"Hi, sweetheart. Is everything okay?" Her mom sounded beat.

"Everything's fine, Mom—hey, I should ask you the same. You sound really tired."

"Oh, it's that nasty flu," her mother replied. "First it knocked your father down for a while, then I guess it decided it likes me better." She let out a sigh, but when she spoke again Zoey could hear the smile in her voice. "Just having you on the phone, I already feel better. So how are things with you, sweetheart? Everything okay at work?"

"Fine, Mom. Listen, can I ask you a question? Dad had a 401(k) at his job, right? Do you have any idea what sort of returns it earned? And what happened to it when he moved to his new job?"

"Oh, Zee," her mother said, "I really couldn't say. Your father looks after all that. You're not thinking of taking that other job, are you?"

Zoey heard the alert tone of a second call coming through. She glanced at her phone's screen. Jessica. "I don't know yet, Mom—listen, I'm so sorry, I have to go."

"Be happy with what you have, sweetheart. The grass doesn't get any greener—"

"I know, Mom—listen, I'll call you tomorrow, I have to get this—love you!"

Zoey ended the call with her mom, but just as she was about to click over to pick up Jessica's call, she hesitated. For some reason she didn't feel like having that particular conversation right now. She let it go to voice mail.

Once she saw the new voice mail alert, she put the phone to her ear again and played the message.

"Hey, Zoe. We're on for Friday, right? Drinks are on me this week! See ya there!—oh, and hey. Did you have The Talk yet with your boss, about leaving the magazine?"

Zoey clicked off the message and set the phone down. "Nope," she said to her empty apartment. "Not yet."

Zoey thought once more (for the hundredth time that week) about that agency job offer. The high-stakes, high-pay, high-pressure job offer. She took a deep breath and let it out again.

Jessica lived in the fast lane, that was for sure. If Jeffrey's strategy was to go for the big break, the zillion-dollar deal, Jessica's was to crank the dial all the way up and plain outwork everyone else. Jessica wasn't bothering to climb the ladder to the top. She was skipping the ladder altogether and *blasting* to the top.

And Zoey? What was *her* strategy?

CHAPTER 6

Don't Budget—Make It Automatic

Thursday morning was bitter cold outside, and despite wrapping her coat tightly around herself, Zoey felt the chill reach into her bones as she fast-walked against the wind. Even so, when she reached the entrance to Helena's Coffee, she hesitated. Jeffrey's words were still echoing in her head. She didn't want to buy into his cynical slant on things . . . but he had some valid points, didn't he? Maybe she should just walk on by and go to work.

She took a breath, pulled the door open, and stepped inside.

She found Henry sitting at his high-top table in the corner, talking with a tall man who might've been a gentleman cowboy from central casting: string tie, pressed white shirt, dark jeans, snakeskin cowboy boots, and a weathered face that looked like a contour map of the Sierra Nevadas.

It was curious, she thought as she waited in line for her latte, how Henry commandeered that corner table, as if it were his official station. It occurred to her for the first time that maybe he wasn't just a barista; maybe he was the morning-shift floor manager. But hadn't Barbara *said* he was a barista?

"Good morning, Zoey," said Henry when he saw her approach with her latte. "Let me introduce you to my friend. Baron's in the energy business."

"Ben Dawson," the man said, shaking her hand, "but my friends all call me Baron. And my enemies are all back in Oklahoma, so who cares what they call me?"

"Pleased to meet you, Baron. Zoey Daniels." Zoey shook his hand. Where Henry's handshake felt like a fine canvas, Baron's felt like buffalo hide. "I hope I'm not interrupting," she added.

"Not at all," said Henry, and he gestured toward an empty stool. "Please. Zoey's a lover of fine photography," he said to Baron as she drew the stool up to the table.

"Henry's been sharing his thoughts on perspective and wealth," said Zoey.

Baron's eyebrows shot up into his forehead. He gave a slow, solemn nod and said, "Aha." Then: "Three secrets? Pay yourself first?"

"Exactly," said Zoey. "Getting rich on ten dollars a day." She grinned.

Baron's eyebrows shot up again. "Ahh-*ha*," he said gravely. He turned to Henry. "You fillin' that poor thing's head with your nonsense, coffee-boy?"

Henry smiled and leaned in toward Baron. "She's already rich," he said confidentially. "She just doesn't know it yet." He glanced back at Zoey and winked.

"Ah," she said. "Well, that's a relief."

Baron chuckled.

Henry cocked his head and looked at her thoughtfully. "Though you do have a question."

Several, thought Zoey. "Seriously, I do," she said. "So I'm not great with structure when it comes to money, as I said. The whole dollar-in-the-jar thing." Henry nodded. "Honestly, I have a hard enough time sticking to an exercise plan. I get the whole 'pay yourself first' idea. But I just don't see myself having the discipline to keep doing that, week after week, for months, let alone years."

Henry nodded. "You probably wouldn't. Which is why there's a second secret." He paused slightly for dramatic effect, then said: "I imagine you've been taught about the virtue of budgets."

Oh, boy, thought Zoey, *here we go.* Zoey hated budgets. She knew it wasn't rational, but something in her rebelled at the very idea of it.

"Budgets!" trumpeted Baron. "Ha! First thing you do with a budget is you take the whole idea, virtue an' all, and toss it in the trash with the rest of the garbage!"

Zoey stifled a burst of laughter. *Yes! A kindred spirit!*

"Budgets!" Baron repeated. "What hogwash." The man was on a roll. He leaned in toward Zoey. "You hate budgets, am I right?" She nodded. "Course you do. Everyone does. Well, not everyone, now: there's such things as people who naturally do well with budgets. Rare, precious creatures, like unicorns. We need those folks, and we give 'em important jobs. Where I work, that's the CFO. He loves budgets. Probably keeps one under his pillow at night. The rest of us mortals? We hate the things, hate 'em like poison."

Zoey was looking forward to seeing how Henry was going to handle *that* outburst and still remain his ever-polite barista self.

Henry just nodded. "He's right, of course."

Zoey stared at him. "Excuse me?"

"Oh, budgets work well enough for corporations and other organizations," Henry continued. "But not so well for individuals. If you have to write a check every week to make your savings plan work, it just won't happen. It's not a measure of character, Zoey.

It's human nature. The idea of a personal budget sounds sensible, in theory, but in the real world, it doesn't work."

"Know why that is?" put in Baron.

Zoey cleared her throat and said, "No. Why?"

"'Cause they're no fun, that's why!" Baron had hijacked the conversation once again. "They're like diets: easy to start and dang near impossible to stick with. Makin' up this list of where all your money oughta go, and tryin' to squeeze your life into all these little pigeonhole categories—it's a *nightmare*. Goes against our nature!"

Henry smiled. "True enough. Which is more or less where I was going with that: no budget is going to make you, 'pay yourself first,' no matter how logical or responsible it may seem. There's only one way to make that happen."

He turned to his notebook and flipped back to the page he'd written on the day before, where underneath the words "Pay Yourself First" he now added a second line in his long, sweeping hand:

2) Don't Budget—Make It Automatic.

"If you have to write a check every week, or keep going online to make regular deposits, sooner or later the thing will unravel. You just won't do it.

"Zoey, let me ask you: Do you consider yourself a busy person?"

"Ha!" said Zoey. "Understatement of the year."

Henry nodded. "Of course you're busy. Everyone is. I'm guessing that the last thing you need is some extra task piled on—like drawing up a budget and then keeping track of it week after week. The truth is, you probably just wouldn't do it."

Zoey certainly couldn't argue with that.

"The only solution," said Henry, "is to take the day-to-day decision out of your hands, by setting up a simple, automatic system that will run by itself in the unseen background. So it takes zero discipline, zero self-control, zero willpower. Just set it up and let it run."

"Can't spend what ain't in your pocket," put in Baron.

"Exactly," said Henry. "That's the beauty of the automatic system. Every two weeks, or every month, or however often you're paid, you set it up with your employer so that your 401(k) contribution automatically comes off the top—which happens *before* withholding comes out for taxes, by the way—and the balanc of your paycheck is automatically deposited into your checki account. That's it."

"It's that simple?" said Zoey.

"It *has* to be that simple. If it isn't, you won't do it. And don't make it automatic, it just won't happen."

"'Make it automatic,'" she murmured, tapping the w her phone.

Baron spoke up again. "The government had this years ago. Up till World War II, all us good Americ our paychecks in full and didn't pay Uncle Sam his following year. Problem was, all us good Americar well. We didn't *budget*." He chuckled. "So they bunch on campaigns to teach us *how* to budge our taxes. And son of a gun—*that* didn't wor Sam said, 'The heck with it,' and set up : pulled out his chunk—"

"*Automatically*," added Henry.

"Automatically," Baron repeated, "b undisciplined little hands. And whadd: time we earned a dollar, *Uncle Sam g*

"And then corporate America got into the game," said Henry. "Do you belong to a gym, Zoey?"

As a matter of fact, she did, treadmills and all.

"Does the gym automatically take a membership fee from your checking account every month?"

She nodded. "They set it up the day I joined."

"Course they did!" put in Baron. "So do most companies these days. 'Cause it works!"

"And that's the second secret," said Henry. "You simply do the same thing for yourself. In fact, the government provided a specific pathway for you to do exactly that—*before* they take out their share for taxes."

"My 401(k)," murmured Zoey.

"Your 401(k)," Henry agreed. "A pretax retirement account. There are other types, too—IRA, self-employment plan (SEP) IRA, and so forth—and other countries have the same idea. They go by different names, with different details, but they all boil down to the same thing: a place where you can pay yourself first, *automatically*, before your income is taxed."

"And with that," Baron said as he pushed back his stool and got his feet, "if you'll excuse me, ladies and gents, I think it's time partake in some of Helena's finest. Anything for you, ma'am?"

Zoey smiled. "I'm fine, thanks." When was the last time she rd someone say "ma'am"?

'Quite the character, your friend," said Zoey as they both hed Baron head up toward the front to go foraging for food.

)h, yes," said Henry. "Resilient, too. Used to be in the oil ·ss, but that industry went through some tough times. he moved to New York, he found a job here with a com- orking in the energy sector, dealing in renewables: wind, id some new technologies, too. Fascinating. Hydrogen,

waste heat conversion . . ." He put a rough twang in his voice and dropped it an octave. " 'Stuff my daddy wouldn't reckonize.'"

Zoey laughed. His Baron impression was excellent.

"Welcome to the future," Henry added. He looked at Zoey. "But you've still got a question."

"Actually," said Zoey, "it's a *few* questions, I guess. If that's okay?"

"Shoot."

Okay, here goes, she thought. Zoey did not want to be rude, but she didn't see any way to get clarity on Jeffrey's objections without just coming out and asking.

"So, yesterday," she began. Henry nodded. "You talked about setting aside some of your income and putting it into an account that gets 10 percent a year." Henry nodded again. "I'm . . . wondering about that. I have a friend who says you can't really get that kind of return anymore. That it's a thing of the past."

Henry smiled. "I understand. A lot of people are skeptical about that. But the reality of it is, since 1926, the first year they started collecting reliable data, the stock market has shown an average annual gain of *over* 10 percent. Sure, the economy booms and busts, we have bull markets and bear markets. How much you actually earn in any given year depends on the year and what you invest in. But when you get past all the drama and look at the big picture, it all averages out. Markets go up, then down, and then up again—*always*. There's never been a market that went down but didn't ultimately go up again.

"After the Great Recession of 2008, people said the days of making money in the market were over. Guess what the market has done since then?"

"Gone up?" said Zoey.

Henry smiled. "With an average annual gain of more than 10 percent."

"Wow," said Zoey.

"Historically," added Henry, "even the most boring, conservative portfolio of stocks and bonds would have earned you a solid 8 percent. But the exact number isn't the point, Zoey. The point is to *save* and let that number compound for you."

"Okay." Zoey thought back to her conversation with Jeffrey again. "But I still get taxed when I take it out, right? So I end up being taxed either way."

"True enough," Henry replied. "But if you keep that dollar for yourself now, instead of giving thirty cents of it to the government, then you have more to invest *now*. Time and the miracle of compound interest have more to work with, so it's going to grow a good deal more. And you don't have to pay taxes on it as it grows each year.

"Here," he said as he turned to another blank sheet in his notebook. "Let me show you."

He began sketching a graph with some numbers and two long curved lines.

A burst of raucous laughter erupted from the front of the shop. Zoey looked up and saw that Baron was regaling the four other customers in line with some story or other. They were all chuckling with him. So was the hipster behind the counter.

Ignoring the scene Baron was making, Henry began explaining his graph.

"Let's say you put $100,000 into an investment that pays an annual return of 10 percent; in thirty years it will have grown to about $661,000. But if you put that same hundred grand into a *tax-deferred* account over the same amount of time, it would come to more than $1.7 million. Nearly triple, in other words."

Investing in a tax-deferred account can make a huge difference!

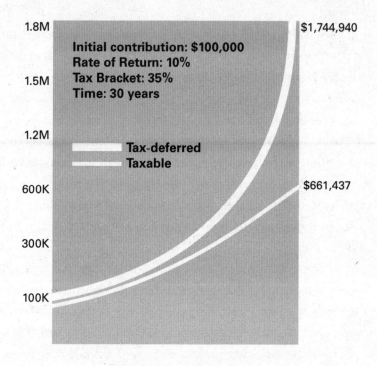

1.8M	$1,744,940

Initial contribution: $100,000
Rate of Return: 10%
Tax Bracket: 35%
Time: 30 years

Tax-deferred
Taxable

1.5M

1.2M

600K $661,437

300K

100K

Difference: $1,083,503

Zoey didn't follow all the math in every detail, but she got the picture, all right. "Nearly triple" was clear enough.

"When it isn't taxed while you're growing it," added Henry, "money grows not just faster but *exponentially* faster. So who cares if you pay taxes on it later, after you've done the growing? If you really want to pay the taxes first, you can start a Roth IRA, where your money grows tax-free forever—*after* you pay taxes on it going in. But if I have a choice between keeping all the money in my account now and paying the government later, versus giving them part of it now? I don't know about you, but I'd rather keep it all now."

Zoey was still staring at the chart. "Why doesn't *everyone* know this stuff?"

Henry shrugged. "That's an excellent question. Sometimes the simplest truths are the easiest to overlook. Or to dismiss as . . . well, as too simple. Not dramatic enough.

"You know that expression about how you eat an elephant?"

Zoey took a sip of her latte and nodded. "One bite at a time."

"Well, that's exactly how you build a fortune. One dollar at a time. But here's how most people *think* you get rich: you win the lottery. You get lucky, and a friend gives you a tip on a new cryptocurrency or great tech stock no one else knows about yet."

Zoey thought of Jeffrey and his surefire plan to launch the next Instagram.

"Or you get an inheritance. A piano falls on that accident-prone great-aunt." (*Good memory*, Zoey thought with a smile.) "Or maybe you find buried treasure in your backyard. And you know what they all have in common? They're all dressed-up versions of the same vague fruitless hope: *Someday my ship will come in.*

"In the movies, sure. But in reality?" He shook his head. "For each person who pulls a winning ticket, there are millions standing in line waiting for the ticket that never comes. Perched on the shore looking out at sea, hoping for that loaded ship to arrive. It's a fairy tale, Zoey—a way of comforting ourselves with a fantasy, perhaps so that we don't have to face the day-to-day reality of our situation."

"Yikes," she said. "You make it sound so bleak."

"Well, it *is* bleak. Bleak is exactly how it works out for a great number of people. It's the financial expression of what Thoreau called 'lives of quiet desperation.'

"But here's the thing, Zoey: *it doesn't have to be.* The truth is your ship is right here, right under your feet. You're standing on the deck. It has already set sail. And you're the captain.

"The question is, what course have you set? And what course do you *want* to set?"

"Here we go," Baron's voice boomed as he rejoined them and set a plate on their little table with two thick slices of some kind of cake, followed by a coffee cup, which he placed in front of Zoey. "Zucchini bread," he said. "Brought you another latte, Zoey. Just in case."

Henry looked up and saw that the line in front now stretched clear to the front door. He got to his feet.

"Will you excuse me?" he said, and he went up front to step behind the counter.

Baron turned back to the little tray he'd set down on the table next to them and now brought out a tiny ceramic cup of something hot. "And a fresh hot espresso, neat, for—"

CHAPTER 7

Big Hat, No Cattle

"Baron!" A petite, elegant woman stepped up to Baron's side and swatted him on the arm. "Are you giving that poor girl a hard time?"

"Zoey," Baron said, "meet my better half. Georgia, this is Henry's friend Zoey." He turned to Zoey and said in a confidential whisper that was loud enough to hear five tables away, "I can't figure it out. She stands around forever, gawking at the same pictures she gawked at last time we were here. Like they might've changed when we weren't looking?"

The woman ignored him and looked at Zoey as she slipped onto Henry's vacated stool. "Baron comes for the gab," she said. "I come for the art. Pleased to meet you, Zoey." She put out her hand and delicately shook Zoey's.

Zoey laughed. "I come for both, I suppose. And the coffee."

"Oh, yes," Georgia agreed. As Baron dug into his zucchini bread, she blew on her hot espresso to cool it. "That Helena. She's something."

"If you don't mind my asking," said Zoey, "how do you two know Henry?"

"Well," said Baron before his wife could reply, "now, that's an interesting story. Musta been, let's see now . . . fifteen years ago?"

"Eighteen," put in Georgia.

Baron shrugged. "Yeah, eighteen, maybe; anyhow, a good while back. Economy was up, oil business was great, times were golden. Living the good life. Fancied myself quite the sharp businessman. King of the Oklahoma fields. Master of the universe. In plain language, I was being an idiot. The real financial brains were over here"—he gave a sideways nod, indicating Georgia—"but I was too stubborn to see it." He tilted his head toward his wife. "Right, darlin'?"

"No comment," said Georgia.

"Down in Texas they have this expression," Baron went on, "'Big hat, no cattle.' All show, it means, and no real assets to back it up. That was me. I got way overextended." He nodded sideways again at Georgia, who was taking tiny sips from her espresso. "And 'cause I dragged her with me, I guess it's fair to say, *we* got way overextended. Economy took a turn. Suddenly the oil business wasn't so great and times weren't so golden."

He looked over at Henry, who was now up front at the counter, busily engaged in brewing coffee drinks for customers. "He tell you the one about how you make a fortune?"

"One dollar at a time," Zoey replied.

Georgia spoke up again. "Turns out, that's also how you *lose* a fortune."

"Yep." Baron nodded, then looked back at Zoey. "That first million, you know?" He shook his head. "It's the toughest to earn—but it's the easiest to blow, and you don't even know you're doing it till it's long gone. Wonder why that is." He shrugged. "Guess it just *is*." He sighed.

"So one day I'm sitting in the doc's office in my skivvies,

and he's messing around with his machines and stethoscopes and whatnot, listening to my heart and such, and he clears his throat and says, 'Baron, I'm gonna tell you something, so listen up, hear?' And he tells me if I don't quit drinking, smoking, and eating ten pounds of hog a day, I'm gonna die.

"I say, 'Don't sugarcoat it, Doc. Tell me how you *really* feel.'

"'Baron,' he says, 'you got a choice here. Your vices, or your life.'

"So I sit there on his damn table, looking at him for a full minute. Finally he says, 'Well? You gonna say anything?'

"'Gimme a minute here!' I say. 'I'm *thinkin'* about it.'"

He threw his head back and roared with laughter, so much so that a few of the customers up front turned to take a discreet look at what the disturbance was. A few others, seated at various tables nearby, just chuckled without looking over. Zoey got the sense that these were regulars who'd all heard Baron's stories before.

"And I *did* think about it, too. Thought about it for a few months. Didn't actually do anything about it, but I thought about it. Mostly what I thought was: *Are you kidding me?* Quit red meat? Quit smoking? Quit the cocktails? Git outta here. Not that I was a problem drinker, especially. Just a problem *everything*. Eighty pounds overweight and eight tons overconfident. It was a contest to see which would collapse first, my credit or my marriage."

"Or your heart," put in Georgia.

"Oh, right. Forgot about that."

"Uh-huh," she said. "Probably forgot about your quadruple bypass too."

He chuckled. "Oh, right," he said again. "That."

Zoey loved the way they played off each other, like a seasoned comedy duo. And these two were old enough to be her parents. When was the last time she'd seen her parents laugh?

"Baron was here in New York on business," Georgia said, "when he had a massive heart attack. By the time I flew up from Tulsa, he was being prepped for surgery."

"Sweetheart?" Having not spoken for a full ten seconds seemed to make Baron antsy. "I'm gonna nose over there and see if I can sniff out a fresh cup of coffee. Zoey?"

"Thanks, but I'm fine," said Zoey.

Baron lumbered off in the direction of the order counter. Zoey turned back to Georgia. "So he was being prepped for surgery," she prompted.

It took a moment for Georgia to go on. "We—" Suddenly Zoey realized the woman's eyes were filling with tears. "We almost lost him. Stubborn old turkey." She laughed and wiped one eye with her tiny coffee napkin. "And he wouldn't listen to anyone. Not the doctors, not his wife, not even our daughter." She took a deep breath and then a sip of her espresso. "But he listened to Henry."

"To *Henry*?" Zoey was trying to picture how the hospitalized Oklahoma oil tycoon and Brooklyn coffee shop morning-shift manager would have crossed paths.

"Yes," said Georgia. "We couldn't travel home, of course, not right away. Even after Baron was out of the hospital, we had to stick around for a while. 'Don't make any plans to leave town,' as they say in the movies." She gave another quiet laugh. "We started poking around the Brooklyn art galleries. Stopped in here one day for coffee, stayed for the photographs on the walls. Met Henry. He and Baron hit it off. And right away Henry started talking sense into him."

"About money?"

Georgia smiled. "About food. Lifestyle. Survival, really. I remember the first time he said, 'You build your health the same way you build your wealth, Baron.'"

The two women spoke the next line together in unison:

"*One bite at a time.*"

Georgia gave her a warm smile. "And Baron actually *listened.*" She shook her head. "Thank heavens for minor miracles. The money part came soon enough, though. Specifically, after we got the hospital's final bill. Now, that nearly put *me* in the cardiac unit." She looked at Zoey. "Did I hear Henry say, 'You're already rich, you just don't know it yet'?"

Zoey nodded, thinking, *Wow.* This woman heard *everything.*

"Well, for us it was exactly the opposite. We were already *broke* and just didn't know it yet. Sure found out, though."

She paused for another tiny sip, then looked at Zoey again.

"I had no idea how overextended we were. I'd always let Baron handle the finances. It wasn't until he was flat on his back in post-op that I started opening the mail myself and seeing where things stood. Which was that we were just about wiped out. All our homes deeply mortgaged. String of maxed-out credit cards as long as the Ozarks—and we'd been making nothing but the monthly minimum payments."

Zoey flinched. Making minimum monthly payments—that was the patented Zoey Daniels method for credit card management.

"I knew this was bad," Georgia continued. "What I couldn't understand was how we'd gotten to that terrible place. One day Henry explained it to me. 'Georgia,' he said, 'if you owe $20,000 in credit card debt and you're only making the minimum monthlies, it will take you more than eighteen years to pay off your balance—at a total of more than $46,000.'

"I nearly fainted. That was more than twice what we'd put on that card in the first place!"

"Wow," said Zoey.

"And that was just one card," said Georgia. "To reach the hole *we* were in, you have to multiply that by several orders of magnitude. The miracle of compound interest. You've heard Henry talk about that, too, I imagine?"

Zoey nodded.

"Well, it cuts both ways. It'll work for you, but it can just as easily work against you. Debt can compound, too, and once it starts, it can grow pretty fast and get pretty scary." She shook her head. "I'd thought we were doing fine. We weren't. We were *very* big hat—*very* no cattle."

Zoey's mind jumped back to that strange ad image she'd seen on Monday morning of the boat stranded in the desert.

If you don't know where you're going, you might not like where you end up.

"So, what did you do?" she said.

"Well," said Georgia, "Henry helped us figure it all out, bit by bit. Sold off our ridiculous mansion in Tulsa and both vacation homes. Didn't get much out of the sales, once all the loans were paid off, but at least it was something. The balance left us just enough for a small down payment on a little condo here in Manhattan. We never did go back to Oklahoma. And bit by bit, we started rebuilding.

"When Baron quit smoking, we discovered it paid, as Baron put it, *unanticipated dividends*. Not only did the man not die, it also knocked quite a chunk off our monthly expenses." She laughed. "You've heard Henry talk about his *latte factor*?"

Zoey nodded—and made a mental note to herself to ask Henry about that. She *still* didn't know what it meant.

"Well," continued Georgia, "Baron called it his *cigarette factor*. And the cigars!" She waved her hand in front of her face as if blowing away a cloud of noxious fumes. "When he quit those, he felt like a new person within a month. The hacking and coughing went away—and there was one more leak plugged in the hull of our money boat.

"We stopped using our cards. Took a few years to pay them off, but we did. Started buying only used cars. My momma used to say, 'When the going gets tough, the tough have cash.'" She smiled. "That was her motto: 'Buy used—and pay cash.'"

She took one last sip of espresso, then set her empty little ceramic cup down.

"Tell you what else," she said. "Henry not only saved our finances, and probably Baron's life, too, but he also saved our marriage. Because we started talking about money. Not arguing about it—actually *talking* about it. Figuring it out together.

"Money just about tore us limb from limb. And money became the glue that put us back together.

"You married, darlin'?" Georgia asked. Zoey shook her head. "Well, remember this for the future: money is the biggest reason marriages fail—but it's not money itself, and not even the *lack* of money. It's the lack of talking about it and working it out *together*.

"I will never forget the first day we sat down and had our first honest talk about money, about our lives and our future. About what we both truly wanted and what steps we needed to put in place to get there. At the time, we were broke as church mice. But sitting there at our kitchen table, talking with him, heart to heart?"

She smiled.

"As far as I was concerned, I was the richest woman in the world."

They were quiet for a moment.

"Anyhow, we've been coming to Henry's place ever since. Not long after we met, Henry made a good-sized investment in the energy company where Baron works, and now the two are constantly gabbing about some new technology or other— What? You okay, darlin'?"

Zoey suddenly looked as if she'd heard a gunshot. *A good-sized investment,* Georgia had said. A good-sized investment? *Henry?* Zoey's mind was racing. "Wait. You said, you've been coming to *Henry's* place ever since? You mean Henry *runs* this place?"

Georgia reached out and patted Zoey's hand. "Darlin', Henry *owns* this place. He started it."

"Georgia?" It was Baron, back at their table and tapping the face of his wristwatch with his forefinger.

"Right," said Georgia, getting to her feet. "Have to meet our daughter at the airport. Next week, Henry!" she called out as the couple made for the door. "So nice to meet you, Zoey!"

Staring motionless at her latte, Zoey didn't even look up.

CHAPTER 8

Myths of Money

Riding the L train to work, Zoey's brain was abuzz.

How did she ever get the idea that Henry was simply working there as a barista? Didn't Barbara say that? She reviewed their Monday lunchtime conversation. No, what Barbara said was, *the older guy you see in there, in the mornings, making the coffee.* That was it. It was Zoey herself who'd made the assumption that Henry was an employee, based on all the times she'd seen him puttering around behind the counter, making people espresso drinks. And he didn't *act* like he owned the place.

Barbara must have *known*, though, right? Why didn't she mention it? And what was her point in pushing Zoey to go talk to him? She felt like chasing her boss down the moment she got to work and asking her.

But she didn't. In fact, once she arrived at the thirty-third floor, she went out of her way to avoid all contact with Barbara.

It was Thursday, and Zoey had not talked with her boss since Monday. That was no accident. She didn't want to be evasive, but she dreaded the idea of having The Talk—the one about her leaving to take that new job at Jessica's media agency uptown.

Not that she'd actually made the decision yet. Which was why she'd been avoiding Jessica as well. Though she had to admit, it really did seem too golden an opportunity to pass up. She was tired of the feeling of running in circles, never getting ahead, seeing no end in sight. (She was even dreaming about it, for heaven's sake!) And those school loans didn't feel as if they were getting any smaller each month. If anything, they felt like they were growing larger.

Which made her think of what Georgia had said about how "the miracle of compound interest" cut both ways: *Debt can compound, too, and once it starts, it can grow pretty fast and get pretty scary.*

Ha, thought Zoey. *Tell me about it.* Although Georgia and Baron certainly seemed like they'd turned things around for themselves, didn't they, and in a big way. Based, at least in part, on advice from Henry!

Which she could appreciate, because he did seem to have a lot of answers. Still, there was something missing in everything he'd said, something that didn't quite fit. And whatever it was, it was nagging at her.

And so her thoughts went, round and round, as she shaved sentences and shaped paragraphs and put in place the final puzzle pieces for their spring issue.

"Are we hungry yet?"

Zoey swiveled on her chair to face Barbara. Was it past one already?

"Thanks, Barbara, but I think I'm going to pass." She had a protein bar in her top desk drawer; that would have to do it for today.

"Your call," said Barbara.

Zoey bent over her work again. About a minute later, she glanced back up over her shoulder. Barbara's face was still there, looking at her.

"So. You talk with Henry?"

Zoey sighed. "In fact, I have. Barbara, why didn't you tell me he *owns* the place!"

"That's *his* business," Barbara replied. "Not mine. And anyway, you didn't ask."

"Very funny." Zoey thought for a moment, then said, "Why exactly were you pushing me into talking to him?"

Barbara shrugged. "Like I said, he sees things differently. You were going on and on about not being able to afford things, and frankly it was getting old."

Zoey laughed and noted a slight twinkle about her boss's eyes—about as close as Barbara ever got to laughing herself.

"Besides," Barbara added, "I didn't push you. Nudged, maybe."

"Noodge," replied Zoey.

"Ha." Barbara paused, then said, "So?"

"So, what?"

"So what do you think about all that stuff Henry's no doubt been telling you the past few days?"

Zoey sighed. "I don't know, Barbara." She looked at her laptop, then turned back to face her boss again. "I'm . . . not really great with money."

Barbara came around to the front of the half partition, leaned back against it, and shook her head slowly. "Zoey, Zoey."

"What," said Zoey, trying not to sound defensive.

"Look," said Barbara. "Normally I make it a rule not to stick my nose into my team members' private lives. But I'm going to tell you something every woman needs to hear. Okay?"

"Okay, boss," said Zoey.

Barbara *hated* being called "boss," but she didn't take the bait. "I'm serious here. You listening?"

"I'm listening," said Zoey.

Barbara came over and perched herself on the corner of Zoey's desk. "The myths of money," she said. "This is what they didn't teach you in journalism school, and they don't teach it in business school, either." She glanced down at Zoey's desk. "You taking notes?"

Zoey turned to her open laptop again, sat with both hands poised to type, and looked back up at Barbara. "The myths of money," she repeated. "What they don't teach you in school."

Barbara nodded. "Okay, then. First is the idea that making more income will make you rich."

Zoey opened a new file and typed a boxed headline:

MYTH #1:
Make more money and you'll be rich.

"Henry probably talked about this already, right?" said Barbara. "How much you earn has almost no bearing on whether or not you'll become financially solid.

"Most people *think* they have an income problem. They don't. They have a spending problem. Don't get me wrong, a healthy income is a thing of beauty. But chasing after the bigger dollar is not necessarily the solution to your money problems."

As she typed, Zoey struggled not to reveal anything on her face. Guilt, for instance. Did Barbara somehow *know* she was considering that job uptown? It was possible. The New York media world was like high school: everyone knew everyone else's business.

"When you grow your income bigger," Barbara continued, "you

just take whatever money problems you have and make *those* bigger, too. Because your money problems come from your money *habits*, and those don't change just because your income goes up. The solution to your money problems isn't more money; it's new habits.

"You with me so far?"

"I'm with you," Zoey said as she typed. Although she wasn't, not really. She followed the logic of it, all right—but Zoey still could not wrap her head around this whole idea. Her money problem was that she didn't *have* enough! How would making more possibly *not* fix that?

"What makes you financially set for life isn't bigger income; it's smart saving and investing. Which brings us to the second myth: that you need to have a lot of extra cash first. You've heard the saying 'It takes money to make money'?"

Zoey nodded.

"That's not only *not* true, it's *so* not true that it's Myth #2."

Zoey inserted a page break and typed another boxed headline.

MYTH #2:
It takes money to make money.

"'I don't make enough to invest'—you know how many women I've heard say this?" said Barbara. "It makes me want to scream. It's like they're saying, 'Without some big windfall, there's no way I'll ever get ahead.' As if financial security were some kind of exclusive club with outrageous membership fees.

"And none of that is true. You don't need a huge chunk of money to build wealth. Did Henry show you his charts—five dollars a day, ten dollars a day, and so forth?"

Zoey nodded.

"Well, he's not just blowing smoke. Those numbers don't lie.

The power of compound interest is as real as gravity. And for most people who've built financial security, that's exactly how they did it: *a dollar at a time*. It doesn't take a big stake to start with. What it takes is facing the reality of your situation and deciding to *do* something about it.

"And you need to stop telling yourself, 'I'm no good with money,' because you don't have to be a mathematical genius or Wall Street wizard, either. What you need is the capacity to be honest with yourself. Which is a rare commodity these days. But not with you, Zoey. It's what I've always liked about you: you don't BS. You're a consistently honest person."

Zoey felt her face flush. She took her hands off the keyboard. "I get your point, Barbara, I really do. But, I don't know . . . I don't want to feel like my life revolves around money."

"Of course not," said Barbara. "But that's not the idea. The idea is to set yourself up so your life won't revolve around the *lack* of money. Which, by the way, no one else is going to do for you.

"Because here's the thing, Zoey, and this is the next myth, maybe the biggest one of all: the idea that when the chips are down and times get tough, someone else—a husband, advisor, big handsome knight galloping up on his mighty steed, *whatever*—that someone other than your own sweet self is going to take care of you and be your safety net. That someone else will take care of you."

Zoey typed.

MYTH #3:
Someone else will take care of you.

"Not that people actually say this out loud," Barbara went on, "because most don't—but they're saying it with their choices and behavior. 'My boyfriend, my husband, my father, my financial advisor, takes care of my finances.' Or: 'Oh, it'll all take care of itself.' I've got news for you: No he doesn't, and no it won't."

Zoey thought about Georgia Dawson saying, *I had no idea how overextended we were.* About her own mother saying, *Your father looks after all that.*

"There's no Prince Charming coming with a big bag of cash. You have to be your own Prince Charming, Zoey.

"And by the way, this is just as true for men as it is for women. The world is full of men who expect that someone—their lawyer, their broker, their company, the next US president—someone else is going to watch out for their financial future. And it's simply not true.

"Your wealth is exactly like your health. Your health doesn't just *happen*; it's not something that takes care of itself as you go through life. You can't leave your health in someone else's hands, and the same goes for your wealth. They're both completely in *your* hands. No one else's."

Zoey finished typing and considered all that for a moment. She looked up at Barbara. "But you did say this is something every *woman* needs to hear."

Barbara nodded. "Let me tell you about us. About women.

"In this enlightened world of ours, women still earn on average 20 percent less than men. Women are hurt more than men are by corporate downsizing, spend about ten more years out of the workforce handling responsibilities such as child-rearing and caring for elderly parents, as a result accumulating 34 percent less in their retirement accounts than men, and their Social Security benefits are significantly lower. And yet, get this: since women live on average about seven years longer than men, and half of all marriages end in divorce, the odds are strong that any given woman will end up spending her "golden years" on her own. Eighty percent of married men die married; 80 percent of married women die widowed! And four out of five widows living in poverty were *not* poor . . . until their husbands died."

She paused to let Zoey's typing catch up.

Zoey wasn't even sure why she was taking all this down. It sure was depressing. It made her think again about her mom, about how tired she always seemed these days, the recurring backaches she hadn't even mentioned (but Zoey's father had, in another rare phone moment), and now that flu she couldn't seem to shake. How on earth would *she* manage if Zoey's father were gone?

"You're following me?" said Barbara.

Zoey looked up. "Um, yeah. It's not what you'd call a subtle point."

"No," said Barbara, "and it isn't pretty, either. But it's important. I know it's hard for you to see this now, in your twenties. The concept of 'retirement' still seems a lifetime away. None of it seems real, I know. But it truly does go by in the blink of an eye. And far too many women suddenly wake up one day to find themselves alone, broke, all their options behind them, and thinking, 'How the hell did I end up *here?*'"

Zoey's mind flashed once more on that Monday morning image on the West Concourse wall, of the ship beached in the desert. She could imagine the captain of that ship asking himself the very same question.

After Barbara left her to her work, Zoey had been bent over her desk for only about an hour when it hit her: the thing that had been bugging her. She realized she did have one more question for Henry. It was so obvious, she practically slapped herself in the forehead.

She'd asked the man a handful of questions that morning.

About whether 10 percent interest was a realistic expectation. About taxation. But those were really *Jeffrey's* questions, not hers. And concerning Jeffrey's biggest objection, the *He's a seventy-year-old barista, what does he know?* question . . . well, Georgia had certainly cleared that one up, hadn't she. The man wasn't a barista after all: he owned the place. And his little dissertation on "making it automatic" seemed to handle Zoey's own concerns about whether she'd ever have the discipline to "pay herself first" for any length of time.

Yet none of those were what was really bugging her.

She needed to talk to Henry again.

What had the kid at the coffee shop said the day before, when she dropped in on her way back home? *Whenever he wants. Usually around three, but could be later. Or earlier.*

She glanced at the clock on her laptop's menu bar. Two fifteen. Could she still catch him? Maybe—if she tore out of there immediately.

Zoey didn't understand her own sense of urgency. What did it really matter? But make sense or not, she needed to ask that question and hear his answer. And she needed to do it *now*.

She popped her laptop into her bag and dashed over to Barbara's office to let her boss know she was leaving early. "Something's come up!" she called out behind her as she made for the elevator.

CHAPTER 9

The Latte Factor

She reached Helena's Coffee just as Henry was walking out the door.

"Well, well," he said. "And to what do I owe this unexpected honor?"

"I – have – a question," said Zoey, still winded from her six-block jog.

"Of course," he said. He looked back at the door behind him, then beyond Zoey toward the corner she'd just crossed, then back at her. "Join me in a coffee?"

Zoey was about to say *Please* and follow him back into Helena's—but instead he set off at a brisk pace down the street. She followed. When he reached the corner he turned, then stopped at the first door and opened it for her.

They were at a Starbucks.

Zoey hesitated and looked at him. *Really?*

"After you," he said with a smile.

They stepped inside and over to the order counter.

"Tall double-shot latte, please," said Zoey. Then added, "Can you make that half decaf?"

"A hot tea, if you would," said Henry. "English Breakfast."

He paid for his tea and Zoey's latte (she objected, but he insisted; *old-school*, she thought with a smile) and they took a small table in back.

"I don't know," said Zoey. "Sitting with you, at a Starbucks. Seems weird. Sacrilegious."

Henry laughed. "Does it?"

"Well," she said, sipping at her latte. "I suppose it's good to know your enemy." She tapped her paper coffee cup against his paper teacup in a soundless toast. "Here's to reconnaissance in the belly of the beast."

Henry gave a cryptic smile. He dipped his tea bag in the boiling hot water a few times.

"I have a confession," said Zoey. "Yesterday, before I learned that you *own* your coffee shop, I was tempted to ask you, 'How on earth does a barista know the "secrets of financial freedom"?'"

Henry squeezed the excess water out of the tea bag and set it to the side, then looked at Zoey with a serious expression. "You mean, if all this 'pay yourself first' stuff actually worked, what is a guy like me doing in his seventies, still working retail?"

Zoey blushed and looked down. "No, I mean . . ." She looked up at him again and gave a rueful smile. "Yes, I guess. More or less."

Henry grinned, then blew on his tea to cool it. "I should give you a little background. When I started Helena's, more than thirty years ago, I had all sorts of friends in this neighborhood. They're all gone now . . ."

"I'm so sorry," Zoey began, but Henry just chuckled.

"No, no," he said, "they didn't *die*. They moved. Or went out of business. You know why I'm still here? Why my business survived?"

"Because the coffee is so good?" said Zoey. "No, not just that; it's the ambience." When Henry smiled that cryptic smile again, she added, "Um, a loyal clientele who loves you?"

Henry laughed. "That's very nice, thank you. But no. I'm still here because *I bought the building.*"

"You bought the building," Zoey repeated.

"And the building next door," Henry added. "And then a few more down the street."

Zoey was at this point stunned into speechlessness. She certainly was revising her picture of "the eccentric barista," wasn't she!

"There are basically two kinds of people, Zoey. Everyone spends money every day, and as they do they're building wealth. *Everyone* builds wealth. The only question is: For whom?

"You mentioned that you rent. When you rent, you are letting life happen to you. When you own, you take a hand in directing the events of your life. When you own your home, you're taking ownership of your life. Or, in my case, of my business.

"For example, Starbucks. When they showed up, everyone thought it was a joke and wouldn't last. Fancy, expensive coffee? Ha. But it lasted, all right, and it grew. Soon the other neighborhood coffee shops were losing business. All my friends got upset. They tried to fight it. They lobbied against it. Campaigned against it."

He paused. Zoey knew a setup for a punch line when she heard it. "And you?" she prompted.

Henry smiled. "I bought stock."

She put her coffee down and stared at him. "Wait. Stock in Starbucks? *You?*"

"Me. While everyone else was either coming in to buy their coffee, or staying away to boycott their coffee, I bought stock in their company. Taking ownership of the situation, you could say."

"Stock in Starbucks," Zoey repeated.

Henry leaned in closer and tapped the table with his forefinger to punctuate his next point. "If you had bought, say, $1,000 worth of Starbucks stock when it went public in 1992, you know what it would be worth today?"

"No idea," said Zoey.

"Nearly a quarter of a million."

"Wow," she said. "You really are consorting with the enemy."

Henry laughed again. "Well, you could see it that way. Here's how I see it. Every time someone comes in here and buys a cup of coffee, two things happen. They're renting a tiny piece of this business. A coffee cup's worth. And, since I own a piece of Starbucks, I'm getting a little bit richer."

Zoey thought about what he'd said. "Two kinds of people."

Henry nodded. "Exactly. Renters and owners. And the beauty of it is, you get to choose which, anytime you want.

"When you pay yourself first and put that dollar—or ten dollars, or twenty-five dollars—toward buying a home, or a business, or stock in a business, or investing in your own future in any way, you are taking ownership of your life.

"Most people lease and loan their lives. Pay yourself first and make it automatic so that you'll keep on doing it, month after month, year in and year out, and you *own* your life."

"Or in your case," added Zoey, "your business."

He nodded. "When I bought that building, I saw it as an investment in my neighborhood, as well as in my business. In the years since, it's gone up well over $1 million in value. But here's my point: How did I buy that building in the first place? Because

I can promise you, I did not win the lottery, or write a hit song. Or find buried treasure in my backyard."

"And you didn't bump off your rich great-aunt?"

Henry smiled. "No, no rich great-aunt to dispatch. No, Zoey, I *built* it, over time, by paying myself first."

Zoey looked thoughtful. Henry could see that something was bothering her.

"Which brings us to your question," he prompted.

"Yes." She hesitated. "I was looking at that chart again. The one that starts with $25 a day that I'm supposedly putting into that savings account, and that adds up to more than $3 million in forty years? Where is that $25 supposed to *come from*?"

"Ah," said Henry. He blew on his tea again, then took a careful sip.

"You say making more income isn't the answer," Zoey went on. "But then you say we're supposed to peel off an extra *10 percent* of my paycheck. More, actually, if you really mean that one-hour-a-day thing, because one-eighth is actually more than *twelve* percent. Which is all great in theory—but how's that supposed to work when I'm already stretched to the limit?"

Henry nodded. "This, Zoey," he said, "this is where the *latte factor* comes in."

Ah. Finally, they were going to talk about that latte factor! Without realizing she was doing it, Zoey sat up straight in her chair.

Henry reached into his pocket, pulled out a five-dollar bill, and set it on the table between them. "Remember this?"

"Five dollars a day," she said. "The miracle of compound interest."

"Exactly," said Henry. "Now let's apply that same idea to your coffee."

Zoey looked at the half-decaf latte in her hand, then back at him. "My coffee."

"Your coffee," said Henry. "That cost, what, four bucks?"

"Four fifty," said Zoey.

"Okay. Seems like an innocent, entirely insignificant thing, right? But watch, when the power of compounding kicks in. Let's say you diverted that 'insignificant' four fifty into a Zoey's Photograph Account. Five days a week, for a year. Without even factoring in any interest at all, in one year you'd have . . . well"—he cocked his head, calculating—"you'd have nearly $1,200." He looked at her. "Do you remember what the price tag was on your print?"

She did. It was exactly $1,200.

Zoey stared at her latte, then back at Henry again. When she spoke, her voice was husky with emotion. "You're saying in a year's time I could *buy* that print—with this *latte*?"

Henry took another sip of tea.

"Whoa," she said. "That's one strong cup of coffee."

He chuckled. "And that, Zoey, is the *latte factor*."

"The miracle of compounding coffee," she murmured.

He raised his tea in another toast, tapping it lightly against her latte. "Here's to your print of Mykonos, gracing your living room wall."

Zoey sat for a moment, thinking. Then she said, "So, goodbye, morning latte?"

Henry's smile faded. He set his tea down, put both palms on the table, and looked at her. "Zoey," he said. "Please don't misunderstand what I'm saying. No, I'm not saying you have to stop drinking lattes. It's not about your coffee. The latte factor is a *metaphor*. It could be anything you spend extra money on that you could happily do without. Cigarettes. A candy bar. Fancy cocktails. Anything.

"The latte factor isn't about being a penny-pincher or denying yourself. It's about getting clear on *what matters*. It's about the little daily extravagances and frivolities, whatever they may be — the five, ten, twenty dollars a day that you could just as easily redirect toward your own future. From *spending* on yourself to *paying* yourself first. It's about giving up something small to get up to something big.

"The point isn't that you can't spend money. Of course you can, and you should. Life is to enjoy. You can buy yourself whatever things you truly want. A nice outfit, a dinner out, a show in town. As long as you 'pay yourself first.'"

Zoey shook her head slowly. She was still looking at the coffee cup in her hand and picturing that big gorgeous framed print on the coffee shop wall, trying to connect the two in her mind.

"Here," said Henry. "Would you do something for me? Just walk me through your day. A typical day. Today, for instance. What did you do, first thing upon leaving your apartment?"

"Got a double shot at Helena's," she said softly. "My $1,200 latte."

"And?" He pulled out his drafting pencil and made a brief notation on a napkin. "Just the latte, or anything with it?"

She arched an eyebrow at him. "No, not just the latte. I also get a muffin. Carrot cake–raisin, usually, or oat-apple. Whatever looks most nourishing. Always delicious, by the way."

"At two seventy-five, if I recall." He jotted down another number on the napkin. "And we are grateful for your patronage. Then what?"

"You mean, what's the next thing I spend money on?"

"Please," he said.

"Well, the train. That's a few dollars. Also two seventy-five, to be exact."

Henry waved one hand. "Transportation. Not really negotiable. What next?"

Zoey thought back to her morning. "Sometimes I take a break at about ten and go pick up an organic juice at the Juice Press downstairs. Fresh squeezed."

"And that costs . . . ?"

"Seven dollars."

"Seven dollars," Henry repeated, jotting it down. "What next?"

"Well, there's lunch. My boss brings her own from home, but I buy mine at the company cafeteria. That's another . . ." She scrunched up her face, trying to remember what she typically spent on lunch. "Another fourteen dollars."

Henry looked up from his jotted notes.

"And after lunch? Anything?"

"No, that's it." Zoey thought for a moment. "Oh, wait. Plus a bottled water. A dollar fifty."

Henry's eyebrows went up. "Wow," he said. "Pretty highbrow water. Okay." He wrote once again on the napkin, then turned it around so Zoey could see the page. "Let's see what we have so far."

morning latte	$4.50
muffin	$2.75
juice	$7.00
lunch	$14.00
bottled water	$1.50
Total	$29.75

"Do you remember the figure it would take to pay yourself your first hour's worth?" said Henry. "The one that would retire you with more than $3 million in the bank?"

"Twenty-five dollars," murmured Zoey.

Henry nodded. "Well, you're already well past that. And we haven't gotten to your afternoon half decaf yet." He nodded at the latte in front of her. "You know, the one that buys your dockside view of Mykonos."

She stared at the napkin.

He picked it up and handed it to her.

"Your latte factor," he said. "Not that that's all fluff. After all, you have to eat. But if you, say, made coffee at home in the morning, brought a piece of fruit with you? Maybe even brought a lunch? If you could redirect even half that daily tab into a retirement account, that simple shift in habits alone would build you one serious nest egg."

His words reminded Zoey of something Barbara had said a few hours ago.

The solution to your money problems isn't more money; it's new habits.

She took the napkin and stuck it in a pocket. "So I'm supposed to, what, keep track of every little expense? Pore over my list every night to see where I can cut back?" To Zoey, this sounded like the worst form of torture.

"No, no, no," said Henry. "Not at all! The point is not to obsess or keep track of every dollar you spend forevermore. Remember: *budgets don't work*. No, the point of the exercise is simply to give yourself a little evidence—to show you that you *already* earn enough right now to build wealth."

She looked up at him.

"You mean, I'm richer than I think," she said.

"You're richer than you think," he echoed. "Which is true, by the way. You, Zoey, earn enough, right now, to become financially independent. It's just that, like most people, you're letting it drain away as quickly as you earn it. It's like filling a bathtub with the drain wide-open and wondering why it never gets full enough to take a nice hot bath. We dribble away what should be the seeds of a fortune on little things that don't matter, without ever giving it much thought. Grabbing all your coffee out, when you could as easily make some at home. Going out to lunch every day. Bottled water. Extra cable channels we don't watch. New clothes filling our closets that we hardly ever wear. Late charges that could just as easily have been avoided.

"It's not about depriving or punishing yourself. It's about shifting your everyday habits, *just a little*.

"And with that little shift, changing your destiny."

That night, after a dinner of leftover pizza and a fresh Greek salad from Luigi's, Zoey stood in her kitchenette, staring at her coffee-maker, a little espresso machine Jeffrey had gotten her for her last birthday. She had hardly ever used it. But she *could*. Right?

What about at work? Could she drink the free coffee from the machine there, the one with all the different types of coffee blends? She didn't see why not.

And lunch? She thought about Barbara's old lacquer lunch box and sighed. What would Zoey save if *she* brought her lunch to work? The idea didn't thrill her. What would she make, peanut butter and jelly sandwiches?

"Ha-ha," she said to her tiny apartment.

She glanced around at the television. How much did she and her roommate actually spend on those cable channels they hardly ever watched? What was hanging in her closet that she rarely wore? What other junk was piled in there? How much of it had she put on credit cards? How much interest had stacked up on those cards? And if she didn't make every single payment on time (which she did not), then just what *were* the late fees?

Zoey groaned. She didn't want to think about how much everything actually cost. She tilted her head back and spoke out loud to the ceiling. "Could someone else figure this all out for me, please?" Ha-ha again. Myth #3 in action.

She pulled out the Starbucks napkin she had stuffed in her pocket, smoothed it out on the little counter, and looked at the total at the bottom of the column of numbers.

$$\$29.75$$

She couldn't help being curious about just what that would work out to.

She dragged her laptop out of her bag, set it up on the counter, and opened it. She found a long-term interest calculator online that allowed her to tally up what that daily expenditure would add up to, five days a week times fifty-two weeks, deposited into a pre-tax account earning 10 percent annual interest over forty years. Rounding up her daily *latte factor* total by twenty-five cents to get an even thirty dollars, she entered the numbers, then clicked on CALCULATE.

And sat back, stunned.

She ran the numbers a second time. And a third.

$$\$4,110,652$$

More than *four million dollars*.

"It's not real," she murmured. It just didn't seem possible.

She heard Jeffrey's voice in her head: *Where are you gonna earn 10 percent?* Henry had explained that. But still . . . what if Jeffrey was right?

She ran the numbers once more, this time lowering the interest rate from 10 to 7 percent.

$1,706,129

What if even that was too optimistic? She ran it once more, this time at only 5 percent.

$991,913

She stared at the screen, still not believing it. Even at 5 percent, it *still* came to nearly $1 million.

She closed her laptop and tried to picture herself fixing a meal and packing a lunch box every morning before work. Brewing coffee on the thirty-third floor of One World Trade. Could she really "divert" her lunch and double-shot latte and the rest into a rich retirement?

She gave her head a shake, as if to clear out the nonsense.

She thought of her mother laughing and saying, *I can't even make frosting!* Her mother's voice over the phone: *Oh, Zee, be happy with what you have.*

She slipped her laptop back into her bag on the floor.

It occurred to her that she'd been approaching her running conversation with Henry as if it were an article for her magazine. Looking for the big picture, the arc of the narrative. She sighed. That was *exactly* what this all felt like. An article she was editing. Someone else's thoughts, someone else's adventures, someone else's journey.

Someone else's life. Not her own.

Her phone buzzed. A text, from Jessica:

We on 4 tomorrow?

Tomorrow: Friday. The job offer deadline. Drinks with Jessica. A thumbs-up and high-fives all around to celebrate her new job.

The phone buzzed a second time.

BTW, did U talk to the agency yet? Tell me U took the job! :-) :-)

Zoey stared at the little screen for what felt like an hour. Then she gingerly picked it up and texted back:

On 4 tomorrow! :-)

She put the phone down again, got up, brushed her teeth, and got ready for bed, where she lay on her back, staring at the ceiling.

She did not feel :-)

No, she thought, not :-) at all. She wasn't sure exactly why, but right now she felt decidedly :-(

CHAPTER 10

The Third Secret

Friday morning did not start well. Determined to pack a lunch, Zoey had tried her hand at cooking something, a simple Mediterranean recipe out of a column from her own magazine. Her efforts had yielded nothing but some inedible charred veggies and a foul mood that was worsening by the minute.

During the night she'd had a truly horrible dream: the treadmill nightmare again, only this time the treadmill was suspended over a bed of hot lava, and she had to stay upright on the crazily accelerating thing or she would fall and become charred herself. She could feel the blistering heat rising from below. Bits of hot ash swirled around her and singed her hair and face. Finally she let out a terrified shriek, and that had jarred her awake.

Lying there in the pitch-blackness at three in the morning, she'd made a decision.

When the call came in from Jessica's agency later in the day, she was going to say yes.

She would ask Barbara to lunch today after they'd put the spring issue to bed—not at the company café but somewhere out of the building—and tell her then. She wasn't looking forward to the conversation, but it had to be done. Barbara could argue all she wanted that more income wasn't the be-all-and-end-all answer to her money problems, and she might well be right—but let's be realistic: a major bump in salary sure wouldn't hurt any.

She grabbed her bag and stepped out into the vestibule, realized it was pouring outside, stepped back inside to grab an umbrella, then took off for the L train, doing her best to avoid the worst puddles as she plowed through the miserable weather. She'd gotten a late start, and besides, she had no plans to stop and talk to Henry today anyway. Enough of the million-dollar fantasies. In fact, maybe she should skip the latte and breakfast muffin altogether and just get to the next train.

Still, as she walked, she couldn't help continuing to sift through her little mental collection of Henry notes. Her editor's brain wouldn't leave it alone.

At the magazine, she would get pieces that had some good writing in them but whose overall point was fuzzy and hard to pin down. Sometimes the writer had tried to fit too many ideas in. Other times they'd left key points out. Or they'd suggested a solid idea but didn't develop it well or bring it to its natural conclusion.

So, what was the natural conclusion here?

She'd made it nearly all the way to the train station, when she abruptly stopped walking. "Sorry—sorry," she mumbled to a few pedestrians who bumped into her as she stood rooted in place.

How had Henry put it? *Wealth, financial freedom? Not that complicated. It's a simple three-step process . . . I call them the Three Secrets to Financial Freedom.*

Pay yourself first . . . Make it automatic . . . That was two.

What was the third secret?

She did an abrupt U-turn and headed back toward Helena's.

Ten minutes later Zoey's umbrella was furled and standing upside down in the umbrella stand inside the coffee shop's front entrance, and Zoey herself was perched on her stool across from Henry.

"Ah," he was saying. "The third secret. All right." He sat back and laced his fingers around one knee. "So let's talk about what's important."

"Okay," said Zoey. "Tell me. What's important?"

"No," said Henry, smiling and shaking his head. "That's not how it works. *You* tell *me.*"

"I'm not sure what you mean."

"We've been talking about saving for retirement as if it's something that matters . . . but how much does it, really? To you, I mean. Yes, you know it's coming—in a half century or so. To me, my seventies are a fact. I'm living them. To you, though, none of that is really *real*, not right now. Am I right?"

He had a point. As much as Barbara's images of women destitute in their old age had freaked her out, forty years in the future did seem like an eternity away.

"So let's set the retirement question aside, just for the moment. What about your life? What about all the living that happens between now and four or five decades from now? What about your dreams?"

"My dreams?" Zoey shuddered. *Oh, you don't want to hear about those*, she thought.

"Not your nightmares," he said gently, as if he had read her mind. "Your *dreams*. Tell me something you've always wanted to do."

The words popped out before she'd even thought about it. "Learn how to shoot amazingly beautiful photographs."

"Photography lessons." He nodded. "Good."

"Not exactly an ambition that'll set the world on fire," said Zoey.

Henry cocked his head thoughtfully. "Don't sell it short," he said. "Bigger dreams are not necessarily better dreams. A dream is a dream. Sometimes the simplest ones are the most compelling. They're certainly more accessible. Like this one. You want to take photography lessons. So, why not just do it?"

Zoey started to speak, but Henry stopped her with an upraised index finger. "Wait. There's a condition here: you don't get to say, 'I can't afford it.'"

"Okay," said Zoey. She thought for a moment, then said, "Because they cost too much."

Henry chuckled.

In fact, there was a local course she'd badly wanted to take for the past few years. It wasn't that expensive — just under $600 — but she'd never quite been able to scrape together the cash.

"All right," said Henry. "Let's look at this. Have you already got an automatic deposit going to your 401(k)?" Seeing her hesitate, he added, "No, you don't."

"No," she admitted, "I don't. But I *am* thinking about it."

He lowered his chin and shot her a stern look. "I'm going to let that remark go unnoticed."

She gave an innocent smile.

"So," he continued, "now that you have — or *once* you have — a little money going into that retirement account, perhaps what you need is a *dream account*. Completely separate from your retirement account, set up exclusively to fund those lessons. Call it Zoey's Photography Course Account, set up so that you automatically deposit into it, say, a hundred dollars a month. Less than three fifty a day." (*Another latte*, Zoey couldn't help thinking.) "How much does this class cost?"

"About $600," said Zoey.

"Well, then. In six months, you go take the class. Dream achieved. Onward! What else have you always wanted to do?"

Zoey froze. For some reason she couldn't come up with a single thing. "I . . ." She looked at him with both palms raised. "I'm drawing a blank."

"Try this," he said. "Close your eyes for a moment." She did. "Take a deep breath: in . . . and out."

Zoey took a deep breath, then let it out.

"All right," said Henry. "Now think back to a time in your life when you experienced *flat-out, unbridled joy*."

She took a deep breath, then slowly exhaled.

She was in the backseat of her parents' car, heading north. She was seven years old, and they were all going on a road trip together up the coast of Maine.

Now she remembered the three of them walking along the ocean's edge. The scrubby foliage, the eagles wheeling in the sky, the shoreline of big rocks and freezing cold water. Breakfast when they got back to the inn. The tiny blueberries bursting with flavor. And the best pancakes (blueberry, of course) that she'd ever eaten in her life.

"Huh," she said, her eyes still closed. She hadn't thought about that trip in years. She described her memories to Henry in murmurs.

She remembered the three of them going out on a lobster boat. Thrilling to the chop of the dark green waves. The feel of the rough wood in her hand when the captain let her control the tiller for a few minutes. She described it all.

"I'd never been out on the water before," she said.

"So tell me, Zoey," she heard Henry say softly. "When you're there, on that little boat off the coast of Maine, how does it feel? What was it about that trip that you loved?"

Zoey opened her eyes and looked at Henry. His eyes were sparkling.

"It felt like an adventure," she said. "Like we could just take off, go anywhere. It was like flying—that feeling of freedom." She paused, then repeated the word. "Freedom."

She closed her eyes again and thought about the word for a moment.

The Freedom Tower.

Her view every day from the company café: the Statue of Liberty.

"I think, maybe, *that's* what I want," she murmured. "Not just photography classes. That feeling of freedom. I just want to know I can do what I want to do, go where I want, when I want to do it." She opened her eyes and blushed. "I supposed that sounds selfish. Or unrealistic."

Henry didn't blink. "I don't know. Does it? Sounds reasonable to me. If you were put here on this earth to do something special, it makes sense to me that you would want the freedom to do it."

Zoey gave a slight nod. "I guess. Yes, I see that."

"So tell me," said Henry, "when you're on that little boat off the coast of Maine, feeling that sense of *freedom*, what does it bring you?"

She closed her eyes once more—and the moment she was back on the boat, the word leapt unbidden from her lips. "Adventure!" She opened her eyes and looked at Henry. "I never thought of it that way, but that's what I want. The freedom to *adventure*. See things I've never seen. Go places I've never gone."

Henry nodded. "And you work where?"

She gave him a puzzled look, and then her face relaxed into a grin. "Ah. Excellent point." She worked as an associate editor for a travel magazine, polishing the words that described other people's travels.

Other people's adventures.

"And if I may ask," Henry continued in a soft voice, "what *kinds* of adventures? Adventures that bring you . . . what?"

Zoey closed her eyes once more and thought about that. If she could go anywhere, do anything, where would she go? "Not sky-diving or motocross," she said. "Not mountain climbing. Adventures like traveling to see the most beautiful places in the world." She thought for a moment again, then said, "It's not the excitement, exactly. It's the *beauty* of it."

She opened her eyes.

Henry had his steel pencil out, and on a fresh page of his little Moleskine he had just written three words:

Freedom, Adventure, Beauty

"You know why most people don't save, Zoey? Or if they do, they save only a pittance, and nothing really significant? Because they just don't see the point.

"These"—he nodded at the three words he'd written—"*these* are the point. People talk about getting a bigger house, a better car, a vacation home, or just a better salary. But none of those things really matter. It's what those things *bring you* that matters.

"These dreams of yours, Zoey, whether they're short-term, like a photography course, or more long-term, like a trip around the world—these dreams are important. They're more than important; they're like oxygen. Without them, your life suffocates.

"That list is probably not complete," he added. "No doubt

you'll want to revise it, edit it, add to it. But you might think of these as your *values*. These are, you could say, what *matters*. To you, I mean."

He nodded at the page again.

"So here's the question. Are the actions you're taking and choices you're making every day bringing you more of *these*? Is the way you spend your money lining up with what matters to you?"

Zoey thought for a moment, then said, "You mean, is it bringing me *flat-out, unbridled joy*?"

He smiled. "That's exactly what I mean."

Zoey gazed at the list of words. For some reason she thought of her mother's voice: *Oh, Zee, be happy with what you have!* Was she?

She looked at Henry again. "Do you mind if I ask *you* a personal question?"

He chuckled. "Please."

"What brings *you* pure, unbridled joy?"

Henry leaned back and gave her a long look. Finally he gave a small nod.

"Now, *that* is an excellent question." He got up off his stool and said, "Walk with me?" They began a slow circuit of the big space as he talked.

"Thirty-six years ago, a good friend asked me that same question. I'd never asked myself that, and I was shocked to find I did not have an answer.

"I was not an unhappy man. Young architect with a good firm, good prospects, secure future. I liked the work I did, liked the people I worked with. But was it truly giving me *flat-out, unbridled joy*?" He shook his head slowly. "No, I had to admit, it was not. I was toiling away for hours a day to pay for *stuff*—stuff that wasn't bringing me any closer to the life I genuinely wanted to be living.

"So I went to my employer and negotiated a little time off. Packed a bag, booked a flight, and left for Europe.

"At first, I said I was just taking a few weeks to . . . well, to reassess. I called it my *radical sabbatical*." He chuckled. "Turned out, I never did go back to that job.

"My friends said I was crazy—that I was throwing away a perfectly good career. For all I knew, they were right. But for years, Zoey, for *years* I'd been telling myself, 'Someday, Henry. Someday you're going to travel the world, search out the most fascinating, beautiful, remarkable spots on the planet and capture them.'

"So I did. That idea that you should put off your best life until you're retired—it suddenly made no sense to me. I gave notice at the firm and traveled for the next six weeks. When I came home, I took out a lease on a vacant little storefront in my favorite neighborhood, took out a small business loan."

"And started a coffee shop," said Zoey.

Henry nodded. "And started paying myself first. Owning my life. It wasn't too many more years before I owned the building, too. And ever since that first trip, I've taken six weeks out of every year to go see the world. Over the last thirty-six years, I've been to over a hundred countries."

All at once Zoey realized what had been right under her nose the whole time. She felt a shiver go up her spine.

"The photos," she whispered. "These are all *yours*."

Henry looked at her and smiled. "Like I said, that print you're so drawn to? It's my favorite."

They had just arrived at the image of Mykonos at dawn, and now the two stood gazing at it again together.

"I remember the day I took that shot as if it were happening right now, today." Henry's voice was soft, with a far-off quality. "Moments after I clicked the shutter, I turned, put my camera down, got down on one knee, and proposed."

"And she said *Yes*," murmured Zoey.

"And she said *Yes*," Henry agreed.

"Helena?"

Henry smiled. "Helena. Like Helen of Troy, the most beautiful woman in all of Greece. We first met right there, by that dock, just a few weeks earlier. It was that very first trip. My *radical sabbatical*. She came back to the States with me and, well . . ." He paused and spread his arms out in a gesture that took in all the photos throughout his coffee shop, a gesture that seemed to say, *Here she is*.

Helena's Coffee.

"The love of my life," he said. "And I have been saying *Yes* ever since."

Zoey finally understood what it was that had so drawn her to this photo. It wasn't simply the beauty of the scene. It was the beauty of the *moment*—a moment bursting with love and endless possibilities, radiant with golden light.

And now that she thought of it, that was true of *all* the photos there, wasn't it. Each one held a special moment in Henry's life, a moment suspended for all time.

And with her next mental breath Zoey suddenly knew, too, what it was about Henry, what it was she'd been trying for days to describe, that quality that made her want to be around him, that drew not only her but Baron and Georgia and Barbara and so many others. *Something magnetic*, she remembered thinking, *like charisma, but that wasn't quite it*. No, it was a quiet joy, a kind of contentment. He was a person steeped in ten thousand moments, all of them lived richly.

It wasn't that he was resourceful, or old-school, or eccentric, or charming, or clever.

He was *rich*.

Not just *money* rich. *Life* rich.

"So, is this the third secret?" she said.

Henry smiled. "Indeed. Without the third secret, the first two serve no real purpose. Without the third secret, the first two ultimately won't work—because you probably won't do them."

He flipped his notebook back to the page where he'd written the first two secrets and now added one more line.

3) Live Rich Now.

"The first two secrets—pay yourself first, make it automatic—those are the *how*. This is the *why*. Figure out what matters, and follow *that*.

"Live rich now. Not in some far-off future. *Today*."

CHAPTER II

The Millionaire Down the Hall

The day hit with full force the moment Zoey stepped off the elevator on the thirty-third floor. It was the spring issue deadline, and everyone in the office was in a production frenzy. The last cloudburst of bios and captions and last-minute rewrites all clamored for her attention, and she attended to them all, one by one . . . yet, even as she did, her thoughts were on the coming lunchtime conversation with Barbara. She hadn't yet called Jess's agency to formally accept the new job offer, but that needed to happen today—and before it did, she needed to let her boss know she was planning to leave.

It hurt just to think about it.

Finally one o'clock arrived and Barbara appeared by her desk.

The rain had fizzled out, and the sun was clearing the haze and drying the sidewalks. They chose a spot in Tribeca, a few blocks away, with outdoor seating. On the walk over, the two talked over a few thoughts on the summer issue, which was already under way.

They sat, scanned the menu, ordered, and made small talk for a minute or two, their maximum tolerance when it came to idle chitchat.

"So," said Barbara after a few moments' silence. "You wanted to talk about something?"

"Yes," said Zoey. "I did." She hesitated. Broke open a roll and dipped one half in olive oil.

"Okay," said Barbara. Then: "And was I supposed to guess what it was?"

Zoey laughed. "Sorry. No, of course not. I'm just . . . I'm . . ." She stopped, put her roll down, and gave Barbara a helpless look. "I'm a little confused."

Barbara put her hand on Zoey's arm. "Relax, Zoey. It's me. I don't bite. Remember?"

Zoey nodded. "It's strange, all this talk, at Henry's coffee shop, about money and compound interest and wealth. It's got me . . ."

"Upset."

"Yeah," said Zoey. "Upset."

"About what?" said Barbara. "It's just talk, right?"

"Right," agreed Zoey. *Just talk.* "It feels like it's all talking about some other universe. The other day, this oil baron I met? He said something about how the most important benchmark is putting away your first million. And I'm sitting there, nodding away, like, 'Oh sure, my first million, I remember that, I think that was right around when I got my braces off.'"

Barbara snorted with laughter.

Zoey picked up her roll again and held it in her hand without taking a bite. "But you know what I mean? What am I doing, sitting there with this man, talking about millions of dollars? Why am I even in this conversation? That's not my life. I'm never going to be some wealthy person."

Barbara waited for a moment, then said, "Why not?"

"*Because,*" said Zoey, trying not to sound irritated. "Because other people have financial freedom, Barbara. People who can afford to buy way-too-expensive artwork. People who work in swanky media agencies. People on television. The people who read our magazine and travel the world, wherever they want, whenever they want. *Other people*, Barbara. Not me!"

"Huh," said Barbara. Then repeated, "Why not?"

"Why *not*? Because I'm . . . because I have student loans up the wazoo, and can't keep track of my credit cards, and can barely afford my rent. And can't even make a decent lunch without inflicting major damage on life, limb, and property!" Her voice was shaking with emotion now. "Because I'm terrible with money, Barbara. Because I wasn't raised with money. Because I'm *me.*"

Barbara said nothing.

"So you tell me, Barbara," said Zoey. "*Why?* Tell me that. Why *should* I be wealthy?" She realized a few other lunch customers were giving her surreptitious glances, but she didn't care.

Barbara looked at her calmly for a moment, then said softly: "Why not?"

Zoey took a long, deep breath, trying to calm herself. "And I don't even know what it is that I'm so upset about!" Barbara grinned slightly at that, and Zoey couldn't help laughing a little. "What a head case, huh?" she said.

Their lunches arrived, and as the server set them down the two women sat silent, watching the endless current of people streaming by.

After the server left, Barbara said, "How many people do you think have walked by our table since we first sat down?"

Zoey took a stab at the number. "I don't know, a few hundred, maybe? More?"

Barbara said, "Without knowing a single one, I can tell you this: if we stopped a hundred of them at random and polled them all, we'd find that most have little to nothing in savings, and quite a few are drowning in debt. In fact, some of the snazziest dressers you've seen walk by? Carrying a negative balance. Owe more than they own. Some of them *way* more."

Big hat, no cattle, thought Zoey.

"And here's what else I can tell you: You know how many of that same one hundred random sampling are actually paying themselves first, and by doing so have been able to put together a million or more in net worth? Maybe five. That's the national profile: five out of a hundred. One in twenty."

"Is that right," said Zoey.

"It is," said Barbara. "Now: You know how to tell which are which, just by looking at them? Go ahead. Look."

Zoey took a bite of her salad as she observed the stream of people, mostly professionals hurrying from one meeting to the next, intermingled with little clusters of tourists moving like schools of fish from landmark to landmark.

She shrugged. "I give up. How can I tell?"

"You can't," said Barbara. "Neither can I. There's no dead giveaway. No 'type.' No special class or privileged group. There's nothing distinct or remarkable about the ones who are wealthy. They look just like everyone else. They just do things a little differently. That's it.

"If I say the word 'millionaire,' what do you see?"

"Someone who looks rich and spends gobs of money on luxuries," said Zoey.

Barbara huffed a short laugh. "Of course you do. That's what most people think. In fact, typically it's just the opposite. By and large, the wealthy spend their money on things that truly matter to them—no more, no less. It's the *unwealthy* who spend money on frivolous things."

The unwealthy. Zoey didn't think she'd ever heard the term before.

"And the financially solid individual? The millionaire?" continued Barbara. "Could be your next-door neighbor. Your plumber." She took a bite of her lunch. "Your coffee shop owner."

Zoey nodded at that and continued working on her salad. "This is true," she said. "I still cannot quite believe it, but yes. Or my coffee shop owner."

Barbara took another bite and added, "Or your boss."

Zoey glanced up from her salad, then put down her fork and knife. She sat back in her chair and stared at Barbara. Eventually she managed to get out one word.

"What?"

Barbara sighed. "Listen, I don't like to talk about this, so, just you and me, okay?" Zoey nodded. "That stuff Henry talks about? I've been doing all that for decades, since I was old enough to earn a paycheck. Long before I ever met Henry."

Zoey found herself fumbling for words. "You. But who . . . ? How . . . ?"

Barbara went back to work on her plate. "It's just how I was raised," she shrugged. "Your oil baron is right, by the way. The first million, that's a major benchmark. You really feel like you've done something. And you have. By the second, it seems much easier: that miracle of compound interest really does take over."

Zoey's mind raced. Her boss, the editorial director . . . *Barbara? A multimillionaire?*

"But, Barbara," she said, her voice a hoarse whisper. "Why do you keep working here?"

"Why not? I love the work; I love the people. Like you, Zoey.

And every now and then I get to have a conversation like this."
She took another bite of her lunch. "Talk to Dave, in HR. He'll
help you set up your 401(k) and max it out, show you how much
the company will match, all that stuff. You'll retire from this place
rich yourself."

You'll retire from this place . . .

And with that, Zoey came crashing back to earth, the words
abruptly reminding her of the reason she'd asked Barbara to lunch
in the first place. The Talk. Leaving her job to go work with Jessica's agency uptown.

She took a breath, trying to shake off the shock of Barbara's
revelation and dig in to the unpleasant business at hand.

"So," she began, "what I wanted to talk about—"

Her phone buzzed. She glanced at it, purely out of reflex, and
was surprised at the number. "Hang on a sec," she told Barbara as
she put the phone to her ear. "Hi," she said, "is everything okay?"

She listened for a moment, nodding woodenly. "Of course,"
she murmured. "I'll be there tonight." She clicked off the phone.
Looked at Barbara.

"I'm sorry, I have to go. It's my mom."

CHAPTER 12

Mom

All the way to Penn Station, Zoey berated herself. She should have seen this coming. She should have paid more attention.

She boarded the train and began the long trek to upstate New York. *Poughkeepsie, Albany, Schenectady* . . . Her mom had kept saying, "I'm fine, Zee, I'm just tired." She should have known. Of course, there'd been the stress when Zoey's father was downsized, and that exhausting move to a smaller place. That flu, the one she kept saying she couldn't seem to shake. The recurring backaches. *Utica, Oneida, Syracuse* . . . "I'll be fine," she'd said. And Zoey had let herself believe it. She was still beating herself up when her cab pulled up to the hospital where her mom had been rushed after collapsing suddenly at lunchtime that day, on the way to the car with two big bags of groceries. The hospital where they then put her mom through a battery of tests.

It wasn't the flu, and her mom wasn't going to be fine at all. She wasn't just tired, and it wasn't just stress. It was cancer, and her mother was dying. "Pancreatic, I'm afraid," the doctor had said, "the kind that often seems to come out of nowhere."

Although nothing came out of nowhere, did it. "I should have known," Zoey whispered. "I should have paid more attention."

Zoey took a deep breath and stepped through the hospital's big front entrance.

She found the room and slipped in through the half-open door, exchanged tight hugs and murmured words of comfort with her father, then took a chair by the bedside.

"Mom?" she whispered.

Her mother's eyes stirred, then opened. "Sweetheart," she said. She closed her eyes again, then opened them once more. "I shouldn't have tried to carry so many groceries," she said, and she gave a weak laugh.

Zoey smiled and felt her eyes sting. "Shhhh," she said.

Her mom felt for her hand. "Zoey," she said, her voice serious now. "I've always told you to be happy with what you have."

"I know, Mom. And I am, really, I am."

Her mom pulled her closer, her grip surprising Zoey in its strength. "Don't."

Zoey leaned in. "Don't what, Mom?"

"Don't, Zee. Don't settle."

"Shhhh," said Zoey again. "Mom, you should save your strength."

"Help me up," said her mother as she struggled to a half-sitting position against the bed's headboard. She took Zoey's hand once more. "Listen to me," she said. "Don't be content with what you have. I love your father, and I love you, and I am not an unhappy woman." She paused, whether searching for the next words or simply to rally the strength it took to complete the thought, Zoey couldn't tell. "But there was so much more I meant to *do*."

"Mom . . . ," Zoey began.

"Now you hush," said her mother, "and listen. I don't want to die with regrets, Zee. Promise me you won't live *half* your life. Live it *all*."

"Mom," Zoey said.

Her mother squeezed her hand so hard it hurt. "Promise me."

Zoey's vision blurred with tears. "I promise."

Much to the surprise of all concerned (especially her doctors), the next morning Zoey's mother was considerably stronger than the day before.

"Stable," her father announced when Zoey came downstairs to her parents' cramped little kitchen. "Not out of the woods, they were quick to point out. They don't expect *that* to happen. But for the moment, anyhow, doing better than they thought."

She and her dad took turns burning things in the kitchen, alternated shifts at the hospital, and talked deep into the night. Her mom mostly slept.

Through those long hours sitting by her mother's bedside, Zoey had plenty of time to think. She kept returning to her conversation with Henry on Friday morning. When he asked her what was important to her, she came up with *freedom*, *adventure*, and *beauty*.

Now it occurred to her that maybe she'd left something off the list. Something big.

Why had she not spent more time with her parents, these last nine or ten years? Well, she'd been busy. She worked a solid eight or nine hours a day, often more, plus all the work she brought home with her to do at night. But for what, exactly? Where were those hours going? And if they weren't going into building what was important to her, into feeding what mattered, then what was the point?

"That list is probably not complete," Henry had said. "You'll probably want to revise it, add to it." He was right.

Freedom. Adventure. Beauty. *Family.*

On Sunday her dad bought her a bus ticket back to New York City, with a hands-on-his-heart pledge to call the instant anything changed. "We're doing okay here for now. You should get back. You need to get busy."

"Busy, Dad?" said Zoey. "Busy doing what?"

He gave her a long hug, then released her and planted a kiss on the top of her head. "Keeping your promise."

eating wild blueberries from a bucket. "Look!" her mother said, pointing. "*Haliaeetus leucocephalus*," added her father. "American bald eagle." Zoey looked up, shielding her eyes from the sun with one hand—and saw the big bird arcing and wheeling around the top few floors of an enormous tower as it stretched through the clouds and upward toward the sky.

She awoke and lay still on her back. Looking up into the semidarkness, she wondered why it was that her little apartment seemed so *quiet*. It took her a full minute to figure it out.

The place itself was not, in fact, any quieter than usual. It was the noise inside her head that had suddenly gone quiet. That constant unspoken sense of worry. Like a refrigerator hum you get so used to that you forget it's there until it goes *click!* and shuts off, leaving nothing behind but a sudden hush.

She smiled in the semidarkness.

Nothing was different, in one sense. It wasn't as if those automatic deposit accounts had already earned her a fortune in the twelve hours since she opened them. But she *felt* different. Just knowing that they would chug along on their own steam now, month after month, year after year, had made that background anxiety pop like a bubble.

Zoey laughed quietly, then drifted off to sleep. She slept straight through till morning. When she awoke, she couldn't remember the last time she had felt so refreshed. She had slept the sleep of the dead, so to speak.

No, she thought, amend that. The sleep of the *free*.

CHAPTER 13

Freedom Tower

On Monday morning the subway car doors opened and Zoey became a drop in the ocean of commuters as it poured through Fulton Center, carrying her along the gray-tiled passageway and out into the huge open space of the Oculus.

In photography, she thought as she traversed the six hundred feet of pure white Italian marble, *the oculus is where you place the camera. Because you see the picture first, in your mind's eye.*

She passed the freestanding concierge desk with its oversize displays of fresh-cut flowers. Today the selection was all white roses and white Madonna lilies.

Where you stand, and what you see from there, is the key to putting together the right picture. That's what creates the perspective you want. You know what I mean?

"I think I do," she whispered as she walked.

She thought again, for the hundredth time, of her mother saying, "But there was so much more I meant to *do*."

She entered the West Concourse passageway and walked by the enormous LED wall display. Today it showed a huge panorama, a gorgeous purple-and-orange sunrise over some stunning mountain range in the American Southwest.

She paused in her journey just long enough to take in the ad message scrolling across the football-field-length screen.

You know how to make your dreams come true?
You buy them . . . a dollar at a time.

She stepped onto the escalator that carried her two stories up and into the sunlit glass atrium, then walked outside and turned back toward West Street, the sun in her eyes, and faced the building where she worked. She tipped her head back and looked straight up, her eyes searching.

Today she could just make out the top of the building as it stretched toward the sky.

That morning Zoey met with Dave in HR. Right then and there, he walked her through setting up her 401(k). It was easier than she expected, and Dave also gave her a few suggestions for how she could put her new plan into practice. When she got home that evening, she went online and set up two new savings accounts at her bank, which she labeled PHOTOGRAPHY COURSE ACCOUNT and ADVENTURE ACCOUNT. In a matter of minutes (following Dave's suggestions), she also set things up online so that her paycheck would be automatically deposited into her checking account, and two transfers would then go automatically from checking into those two new accounts.

The amounts weren't much, but that was okay. In time she would increase them.

After saying goodbye to her father and boarding her train the night before, Zoey realized how much more she had gotten out of her conversations with Henry than just a new financial plan.

She came away with a new sense of clarity about her life's purpose, about what really mattered to her. She saw now that she, like Henry in his youth, was toiling away for hours a day to pay for things that weren't bringing her any closer to the life she genuinely wanted to be living.

And once she realized that, it occurred to her that it might not take nearly as much money as she'd thought to start living that life. Perhaps it wasn't that she needed to be earning more. Perhaps she just needed to get clearer about what she was doing with the money she was already earning.

On the train ride home she had texted Jessica.

Jess, TY so much for the amazing oppty—but I decided 2 pass. Happy @ Frdm Twr.

The truth was, she *was* happy at her job, loved the work and loved the people there. She just needed to make some changes.

After meeting with Dave, she met with Barbara and told her she wanted to take time off to travel, as Henry had done. To have her own *radical sabbaticals*. It would mean she'd be absent once a year for an entire issue, but she could take her laptop with her and maybe work remotely. Did Barbara think she might be able to work with Zoey on that plan and help make it happen?

After she finished making her pitch, her boss was silent for a moment. Then Barbara gave a shrug and her trademark blank expression and said, "Sure. On one condition."

"Which is?" prompted Zoey.

"That you send me postcards."

That night Zoey had a dream.

She was drifting lazily in a small boat along the coast of Maine,

CHAPTER 14

Mykonos

Three years later . . .

The sun peeked up over the little hills in the distance, its lengthened rays casting an amber-golden glow that sparkled like jewels. Zoey lifted her camera and snapped three shots in quick succession. Then lowered her camera again, and just watched. Rows of tiny whitewashed houses snaked along the cobbled streets, their royal-blue doors and shutters dotting the landscape like flecks of blueberry. A flock of red-beaked seagulls passed across her field of vision. She heard the creak and groan of thick ropes as the fishing boat in the foreground rocked at dockside.

Was she really thirty? She could scarcely believe it. Three years had gone by so fast, like a time-travel hiccup or a trick of the light, and yet so much had happened in those three years. She had become a regular at Helena's. She and Georgia Dawson had become good friends. And her whole life had changed.

Her mom surprised her doctors by hanging on for another six

months. Zoey had made the trek upstate and back a few dozen times to visit her in the facility where she was being attended to, and the two packed more time together into those six months than they'd had in years. Henry called it their "bonus round," and Zoey thought he had that exactly right.

Yet that sweet reprieve could not last forever. When her mom passed away, Zoey's dad sold the home in upstate New York, and with those proceeds and the life insurance settlement as down payment, she and her dad went in on a little duplex in a cozy neighborhood in Brooklyn. *Taking ownership*, as Henry said. Tiny as it was, they each had their own bedroom, which in Zoey's case also served as a little studio where she could write and do some yoga. And study in the evenings for her photography course. Just as Henry had predicted, it took her only six months to save up the tuition.

Paying off the credit cards had taken a bit longer. Once she'd learned how to set up her essential bill payments to go out of her checking account automatically on whatever day of the month she set, she put those credit card minimums on automatic. Not only did that lift another burden of worry off her shoulders, but she was also surprised (and thrilled) to see just how much she saved by not paying any more late fees.

Quite a decent latte factor itself.

Following a suggestion from Henry, she'd soon added a second automatic monthly payment on each card, timed two weeks after its corresponding minimum payment, and the two together were like a pair of sharp axes to a tree: in twenty-two months the tree fell, and her card balances hit zero. No more card payments. More latte factor.

The student loans . . . well, that was a more long-term project. It would take some years. That was okay. She'd get there.

The light was already changing, that amber-golden glow just beginning to pale. More noises from the boat. She lifted her camera again and snapped a few more shots.

The cards and loans weren't the only places where Zoey found her latte factor lurking. The basic math Henry had scribbled on the little Starbucks napkin turned out to be pretty accurate. And, miracle of miracles and with Georgia's patient help, Zoey had taught herself to *cook*. "It's exactly like photography," Georgia told her, "except that when you're finished setting up and taking the shot, you get to eat it." That made Zoey laugh so hard, she almost shot latte out her nose. The amount she saved by making her own lunches, though, that was no laughing matter. Like Baron's *unanticipated dividends* when he quit smoking. His *cigarette factor*, she thought with a smile.

Zoey had canceled the premium cable channels she never watched (*latte factor*) and the gym membership she hardly ever used (*latte factor*). Gave away outfits she never wore and tossed the catalogs that would have seduced her into buying more (*latte factor*). Meanwhile her retirement account began building, and so did her Adventure Account.

The village now began to stir as the sun continued its climb, degree by degree, and she caught fragments of quiet conversation from fishermen readying their boats. Golden Hour would soon be past.

She snapped another photo, then another, and one more, then paused to study the camera in her hands. It was a beauty. An early birthday present from Georgia and Baron, given just days before she'd left the States, since they wouldn't be with her on her actual birthday.

Which, as it happened, was today.

This was the last stop on her six-week swing through the Greek islands. She'd taken notes the whole time, and emailed in her story just the previous day. Barbara emailed her that night to tell her the news: they were running her piece in the next issue—*with* some of her photos—as a feature story! She would be returning to a promotion. Zoey was now not only an associate editor but also a *contributing columnist.* Barbara had concluded her email with this brief sign-off:

> Happy birthday, Z.
> —Boss
> P.S. Nice postcards

This was Zoey's third annual trip—her third *radical sabbatical.* The previous year she had ventured west of the Mississippi for the first time in her life and spent five weeks in the mountains of the American Southwest, from Sedona, Arizona, to Las Cruces, New Mexico. A few of her photos from that trip now graced a wall at Helena's.

Sabbatical #2 had been amazing, but not even the Red Rocks of Sedona could outdo the magic of Sabbatical #1. That first fall, not long after saying goodbye to her mom for the last time, she and her father had spent four weeks together on the coast of Maine. They foraged wild blueberries, photographed bald eagles nesting in the waterways, went out on lobster boats. Told each other stories from years past, reliving moments with Zoey's mom, sharing those living photographs framed in time and captured through the lenses of their hearts. The trip didn't cost that much (which was helpful; Zoey was, after all, still saving for her Greek islands trip), but it was the richest experience Zoey had ever had.

Before leaving for Greece, she asked her father, if he could go anywhere in the world, where would *he* want to go? "Alaska," he replied without hesitation.

"It's a date," she said. "Next year, Dad. Start packing."

She took a sip of her hot Greek coffee and watched as the little village came to life under the Aegean sun. She hefted her camera in her hands again and lifted it to her eye—her oculus—to take another shot.

"*Yes*," she whispered.

Zoey Daniels was thirty years old today, and as far as she was concerned, she was the richest woman in the world.

THE THREE SECRETS TO FINANCIAL FREEDOM

1: Pay Yourself First.

2: Don't Budget—
Make It Automatic.

3: Live Rich Now.

A Conversation with David Bach

David, I understand the deathbed conversation Zoey has with her mother, about living a life of no regrets, is based on the last conversation you had with your own grandmother, Rose Bach, before she died. Could you share her story and how it shaped your life and your work?

My grandmother Rose was a remarkable woman. At thirty she made a decision that would change the destiny of our family forever: that decision was she didn't want to be poor anymore.

At the time, she worked at the Gimbels department store in Milwaukee, Wisconsin, selling wigs. Neither she nor my grandfather Jack had a college education. They were your classic hardworking midwesterners, living paycheck to paycheck. Their life was a struggle. But my grandmother had a dream that their life could be better. So, starting on her thirtieth birthday, she told my grandfather, "It's time for us to fix our lives. It's time for us to save."

Together, she and my grandfather began saving one dollar a week. Literally, one dollar. But she came to work and brown-bagged her lunch. Her friends teased her: "Oh, Rose, you're so cheap! Come have lunch with us!" they would say. She said she was sad, at first, but she knew why she was saving. She wanted out of Milwaukee in the winters, where it was cold. She wanted to one day be able to retire to where it was warm.

Over her lifetime, through saving and investing, she became a self-made millionaire. And she passed her knowledge and love of investing forward—to me. She helped me buy my first stock at age seven (in McDonald's, which at the time was my favorite restaurant in the whole world). She became my first money mentor. Ultimately, her teachings would shape my entire life, career, and *purpose*.

My first book, over twenty years ago, was *Smart Women Finish Rich*, and it was dedicated to her and the lessons I had learned from her. I started writing that book in 1997, and my grandma knew I was working on it. Unfortunately, that year at the age of eighty-six, my strong, healthy grandmother—who walked five miles a day and drank green juice every day, who outlived my grandfather by a decade and was dating three men three nights a week (which we didn't learn about until later on, at her funeral!)—had a stroke.

After her stroke, we moved her from Laguna Beach, California, to a nursing care facility in the Bay Area, a mile from our office and where we lived, so we could visit her every day and watch over her care. I remember those final visits with her as if they were yesterday.

I asked my grandmother if she had any last life lessons for me. She thought about it for a moment, then said, "No, I've shared my life lessons with you. You're going to do great in life."

I then asked her if she had any regrets. She thought about that and said, "No—none." And she went on to list all those things in her life that she was most grateful for.

The next morning I went to visit her again and asked her how she slept.

"Terribly," she said. "I was up all night thinking about my life regrets—thank you very much!"

We laughed together, and then she held my hand as she

walked me through her five regrets, going all the way back to when she was a teen. Then she said, "David, I want you to listen to me carefully now. My personal regrets are not the lesson. The lesson is why I have these regrets.

"At each moment I just shared with you, my life had come to a fork in the road, and I had to make a decision: Do I take the safe route, where I think I know the outcome? Or do I take the riskier route—the one where I hope the real gold lies, but the path to get there is uncertain?

"Do I take the risk to get what I really want?

"At each of those specific moments I just shared, those moments I now regret, I took the safe road. And now I lie here dying, and I will never know what could have happened."

"But, Grandma," I said, "you've had the most amazing life!"

She held my hand harder (even though she was quite weak) and said, "David, don't have regrets later in life. Take the risk.

"And remember this," she added. "When you get to your fork in the road, you will hear two voices: the big-boy voice that says, 'Be safe, go the safe road!' And the little-boy voice that says, 'David, go *this* way! It'll be fun! Let's try!' That voice, the little-boy voice, the one that's excited and wants to play—let that little boy come out and play. And tell your friends to do the same."

That was our last visit together.

I drove back to my office, parked the car in the underground parking garage, and cried deeply for a while. Finally, I looked up in the rearview mirror, wiped my tears away, and said, "I'm done. I'm not going to spend the rest of my life as a financial advisor at a large firm. I'm going to finish writing *Smart Women Finish Rich* and dedicate my life to helping more people in a bigger way. I don't know how, but I promise you, Grandma, that within three years I will be out of this place and reaching for my dreams. I will let my little boy come out and play."

In fact, it took four years, not three. But it happened. Exactly four years from that moment, I left the large financial services company where I worked and moved from California, where all my extended family and friends were, to New York City on a hope and a prayer that I could write more books and help millions of people with my grandmother Rose's lessons on how to live rich and finish rich.

It wasn't easy; in truth it was hard. And many things have gone wrong along the way—but I have no regrets. Much more has worked out well than I could have ever originally dreamed possible. *Smart Women Finish Rich* became a runaway bestseller and today has sold over a million copies. Five years later I appeared on *The Oprah Winfrey Show*, reaching tens of millions with my message.

That desire to have no regrets continues with this book.

For years, ever since that live show on *Oprah* where I taught the Latte Factor on her stage, I've wanted to write a little book like this one that explains the Latte Factor in a simple story anyone can read in a few hours, even those who wouldn't normally read a book on money. But my publisher unfortunately wasn't enthusiastic. Finally, after seven more books and my publisher continuing to pass on my little Latte Factor idea, I decided to write the book anyway and find a new publisher for it. Which is exactly what happened. And now it's in your hands.

When Zoey's mother tells her "Don't live *half* your life. Live it *all*," it becomes the trigger that motivates Zoey to stop living scared, stop living small, and go for a life of richness—which has very little to do with money and everything to do with living a life of no regrets.

The Latte Factor was never about the coffee, and not even about the money. It has always been a metaphor to motivate and inspire dreamers to go live their dreams.

No regrets. Let your "little girl" or "little boy" come out to play. You could start today.

What's next for you? Are you working on another book?

I tend to write one book, then promise myself and my wife (who has learned to ignore me on this) that that was it, I will never write another one. And the moment the book is truly finished and put to bed, often another idea pops up.

So the short answer is yes, I do plan to write another book, and it's going to be a lot of fun—and, again, something completely different.

Within ninety days after we launch *The Latte Factor*, I'll be moving across the Atlantic to spend a year with my family in Florence, Italy. I'm truly committed to living a life of no regrets, and I want my kids to have the experience of living in Italy and extensively traveling abroad before they go to college and are off creating their own lives. So if all goes as planned, by the time you read this, I will be living in Florence, eating pasta, drinking wine, and loving my daily gelato with my boys and wife—and writing another book, this one a memoir about my *radical sabbatical*. Just like Zoey.

I might even blog about it and podcast from there. You can join us on the journey at www.davidbach.com.

You've included some great charts and worksheets here; any additional thoughts on how to use them?

The first thing you'll see are some of my favorite charts that highlight the miracle of compound interest. The first chart, "The Time Value of Money," motivated me to start saving in my early twenties. Then, I've included a chart that shows interest rates varying from

2 through 12 percent (see page 137), so you can see the difference these returns make in how fast your money can potentially grow. Finally, there is a chart that blew my mind when I first saw it in my early twenties, that shows the annualized return of investments dating back to 1926 (see page 138). Don't believe the critics who tell you that investing in the stock market doesn't work anymore!

Following the charts, you'll find a few simple worksheets that will help you take action. The first is what I call The Latte Factor Challenge™. For one day, carry this book with you and track your own Latte Factor. Just one day. Don't change anything about how you spend money. Just be you. Spend like you normally do. Then go back through the day and add up all those expenses that are a Latte Factor in your mind. Run the numbers: Calculate what that daily savings could be worth if you changed just a few small things.

Then, on day two, take the Double Latte Factor Challenge. We don't discuss this in this book, but it's simple: Write down what you pay for monthly, then add that up and decide what you can cancel or reduce to cut your expenses faster.

If this is my first book of yours, which of your other books would you recommend I read next?

Without question, read *The Automatic Millionaire* first. This is the book I tell everyone to start with, and it's my most popular book so far. It's a fast, easy read that will show you what you need to do to become a millionaire—*without* a budget. Next, if you're a woman, read *Smart Women Finish Rich*, and if you're a couple, get *Smart Couples Finish Rich*. These books will help you explore your values, dreams, and life goals and build a personal financial plan to make them real. All three have recently been painstakingly updated in the American editions, so make sure you order the updated versions.

I wish I'd read this book twenty years ago! What if I'm in my forties, fifties, or beyond—is it too late to make the Latte Factor principles work for me?

The short answer is, it's never too late to live rich and finish rich—provided you start today.

I wrote my book *Start Late, Finish Rich* specifically for people in exactly your position, people who've saved too little, or borrowed too much, or got sidetracked by life's unexpected challenges. Starting late doesn't mean you are doomed to an uncertain future. It's never too late to live your dreams. All it takes is the decision to start.

The miracle of saving and investing is that money doesn't know your age. It's just math. Let's say you're fifty and married. Can you personally save $10 a day? Can your spouse or partner? Great; that's $20 a day, times 365 days a year = $7,300. Invest that, earn 10 percent, and in twenty years you've got $461,696—nearly half a million dollars.

Double that, with each of you saving $20 a day, and that's $14,600 a year; invested at 10 percent, and in twenty years that's nearly a million dollars.

The most important part of working on a catch-up plan is to work on it—not worry on it. You are where you need to be today; now is your time to get started!

Any last thoughts? How can people get in touch with you?

Most importantly, thank you for being here and reading this!

One suggestion I would make is that this amazing journey

Zoey grows through is an example of "you don't have to do this by yourself." Zoey finds mentors and makes new friends who encourage and support her dreams and new life. I recommend that you make your own Live Rich Now team—that you find others like yourself who might be inspired to take the Latte Factor journey with you.

A great way to start can be to get a group together and have a reading club where you all read *The Latte Factor*, then get together and talk about it. You can take the Latte Factor challenges together and support each other in your dreams. It can be life-changing when you do this with others you love or find new friends like yourself who want to live a richer life—and do this together.

If this book touches you, please feel free to email me at success@finishrich.com. I can't promise a personal reply, but I do promise to read every single one. I love my readers, and I'm truly touched on a daily basis hearing from them. It's my readers' successes using the Latte Factor in their lives that have kept me on the journey of doing what I do for nearly twenty-five years now.

And please come visit me at www.davidbach.com. There's a Latte Factor podcast on our website that is a continuation of this interview, which you can listen to for more great ideas. We also have a newsletter I write when I feel inspired; it's my way of staying in touch with my readers. It's free, and we don't do the usual spammy thing and bug you with stuff to buy (until I put out a new book, of course *smile*).

Now, go put this little book to work in *your* life.

No regrets!

Appendix: Charts

THE TIME VALUE OF MONEY

Invest Now Rather Than Later

AGE	SUSAN INVESTMENT	SUSAN TOTAL VALUE	SEE THE DIFFERENCE	AGE	KIM INVESTMENT	KIM TOTAL VALUE
	Investing at age 19 *(10% Annual Return)*				Investing at age 27 *(10% Annual Return)*	
19	$2,000	2,200		19	0	0
20	2,000	4,620		20	0	0
21	2,000	7,282		21	0	0
22	2,000	10,210		22	0	0
23	2,000	13,431		23	0	0
24	2,000	16,974		24	0	0
25	2,000	20,871		25	0	0
26	2,000	25,158		26	0	0
27	0	27,674		27	$2,000	2,200
28	0	30,442		28	2,000	4,620
29	0	33,486		29	2,000	7,282
30	0	36,834		30	2,000	10,210
31	0	40,518		31	2,000	13,431
32	0	44,570		32	2,000	16,974
33	0	48,027		33	2,000	20,871
34	0	53,929		34	2,000	25,158
35	0	59,322		35	2,000	29,874
36	0	65,256		36	2,000	35,072
37	0	71,780		37	2,000	40,768
38	0	78,958		38	2,000	47,045
39	0	86,854		39	2,000	53,949
40	0	95,540		40	2,000	61,544
41	0	105,094		41	2,000	69,899
42	0	115,603		42	2,000	79,089
43	0	127,163		43	2,000	89,198
44	0	130,880		44	2,000	100,318
45	0	153,868		45	2,000	112,550
46	0	169,255		46	2,000	126,005
47	0	188,180		47	2,000	140,805
48	0	204,798		48	2,000	157,086
49	0	226,278		49	2,000	174,094
50	0	247,806		50	2,000	194,694
51	0	272,586		51	2,000	216,363
52	0	299,845		52	2,000	240,199
53	0	329,830		53	2,000	266,419
54	0	362,813		54	2,000	295,261
55	0	399,094		55	2,000	326,988
56	0	439,003		56	2,000	361,886
57	0	482,904		57	2,000	400,275
58	0	531,194		58	2,000	442,503
59	0	584,314		59	2,000	488,953
60	0	642,745		60	2,000	540,048
61	0	707,020		61	2,000	596,253
62	0	777,722		62	2,000	658,078
63	0	855,494		63	2,000	726,086
64	0	941,043		64	2,000	800,895
65	0	1,035,148		65	2,000	883,185

EARNINGS BEYOND INVESTMENT $1,019,148

EARNINGS BEYOND INVESTMENT $805,185

SUSAN EARNS	$1,019,148
KIM EARNS	$805,185
SUSAN EARNS MORE	$213,963

Susan invested one-fifth the dollars but has 25% more to show
START INVESTING EARLY!

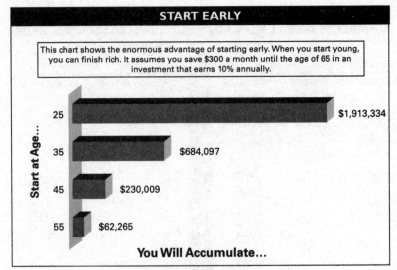

START EARLY

This chart shows the enormous advantage of starting early. When you start young, you can finish rich. It assumes you save $300 a month until the age of 65 in an investment that earns 10% annually.

Start at Age...

25	$1,913,334
35	$684,097
45	$230,009
55	$62,265

You Will Accumulate...

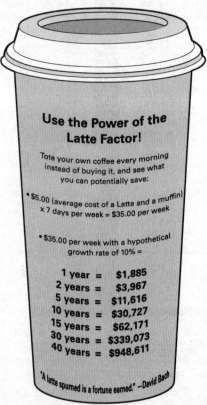

Use the Power of the Latte Factor!

Tote your own coffee every morning instead of buying it, and see what you can potentially save:

• $5.00 (average cost of a Latte and a muffin) x 7 days per week = $35.00 per week

• $35.00 per week with a hypothetical growth rate of 10% =

1 year	=	$1,885
2 years	=	$3,967
5 years	=	$11,616
10 years	=	$30,727
15 years	=	$62,171
30 years	=	$339,073
40 years	=	$948,611

"A latte spumed is a fortune earned." —David Bach

THE EARLIER YOU START, THE BIGGER YOUR NEST EGG
(Assumes 10% Annual Rate of Return)

Daily Investment	Monthly Investment	10 Years	20 Years	30 Years	40 Years	50 Years
$5	$150	$30,727	$113,905	$339,073	$948,612	$2,598,659
$10	$300	$61,453	$227,811	$678,146	$1,897,224	$5,197,317
$15	$450	$92,180	$341,716	$1,017,220	$2,845,836	$7,795,976
$20	$600	$122,907	$455,621	$1,356,293	$3,794,448	$10,394,634
$30	$900	$184,360	$683,432	$2,034,439	$5,691,672	$15,591,952
$40	$1,200	$245,814	$911,243	$2,712,586	$7,588,895	$20,789,269
$50	$1,500	$307,267	$1,139,053	$3,390,732	$9,486,119	$25,986,586

A PACK A DAY KEEPS RETIREMENT AWAY
(Assumes 10% Annual Rate of Return)

A Pack a Day Costs	Over a Month That Comes to	10 Years	20 Years	30 Years	40 Years	50 Years
$7	$210	$43,017	$159,467	$474,702	$1,328,057	$3,638,122

BOTTLED WATER IS A FORTUNE DOWN THE DRAIN
(Assumes 10% Annual Rate of Return)

Avg. Daily Water Purchase	Over a Month That Comes to	10 Years	20 Years	30 Years	40 Years	50 Years
$1	$30	$6,145	$22,781	$67,815	$189,722	$519,732

HOW MUCH MONEY DO YOU NEED TO SAVE EACH DAY TO BECOME A MILLIONAIRE BY 65?			
Daily or Monthly Investments Suggested to Build $1,000,000 by Age 65 10% Annual Interest Rate			
Starting Age	Daily Savings	Monthly Savings	Yearly Savings
20	$4.00	$124.00	$1,488.00
25	$6.00	$186.00	$2,232.00
30	$10.00	$310.00	$3,720.00
35	$16.00	$496.00	$5,952.00
40	$26.00	$806.00	$9,672.00
45	$45.00	$1,395.00	$16,740.00
50	$81.00	$2,511.00	$30,132.00
55	$161.00	$4,991.00	$59,892.00

The purpose of this chart is to share with you how much money you should be saving, daily, monthly, or annually, with a rate of return of 10% to accumulate $1,000,000 by the age of 65.

SAVINGS GROWTH OF $100 DEPOSITED MONTHLY

Depending on the rate of return, putting just $100 a month into an interest-bearing account and then letting it compound can generate a surprisingly large nest egg.

Interest Rate	5 Years	10 Years	15 Years	20 Years	25 Years	30 Years	35 Years	40 Years
$100/mo invested at 2.0%	$6,315	$13,294	$21,006	$29,529	$38,947	$49,355	$60,856	$73,566
$100/mo invested at 3.0%	6,481	14,009	22,754	32,912	44,712	58,419	74,342	92,837
$100/mo invested at 4.0%	6,652	14,774	24,691	36,800	51,584	69,636	91,678	118,590
$100/mo invested at 5.0%	6,829	15,593	26,840	41,275	59,799	83,573	114,083	153,238
$100/mo invested at 6.0%	7,012	16,470	29,227	49,435	69,646	100,954	143,183	200,145
$100/mo invested at 7.0%	7,201	17,409	31,881	52,397	81,480	122,709	181,156	264,012
$100/mo invested at 8.0%	7,397	18,417	34,835	59,295	95,737	150,030	230,918	351,428
$100/mo invested at 9.0%	7,599	19,497	38,124	67,290	112,953	184,447	296,385	471,643
$100/mo invested at 10.0%	7,808	20,655	41,792	76,570	133,789	227,933	382,828	637,678
$100/mo invested at 11.0%	8,025	21,899	45,886	87,357	159,058	283,023	497,347	867,896
$100/mo invested at 12.0%	8,249	23,234	50,458	99,915	189,764	352,991	649,527	1,188,242

WHO SAYS YOU CAN'T EARN 10%?

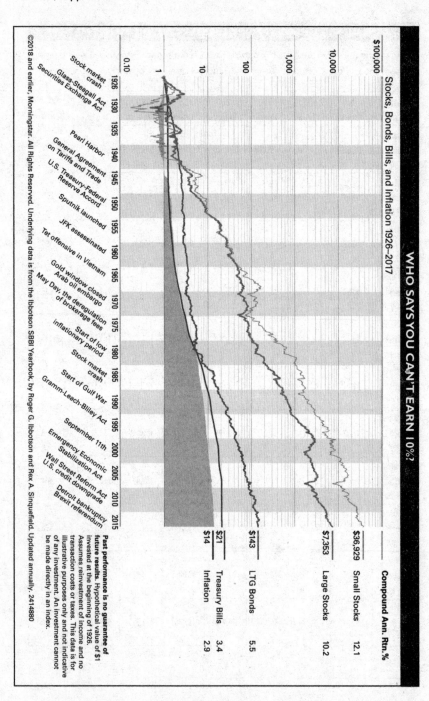

Stocks, Bonds, Bills, and Inflation 1926–2017

	Compound Ann. Rtn.%
$36,929	Small Stocks	12.1
$7,353	Large Stocks	10.2
$143	LTG Bonds	5.5
$21	Treasury Bills	3.4
$14	Inflation	2.9

Events (left to right):
- Stock market crash
- Glass-Steagall Act
- Securities Exchange Act
- Pearl Harbor
- General Agreement on Tariffs and Trade
- U.S. Treasury-Federal Reserve Accord
- Sputnik launched
- JFK assassinated
- Tet offensive in Vietnam
- Gold window closed
- Arab oil embargo
- May Day, the deregulation of brokerage fees
- Start of low inflationary period
- Stock market crash
- Start of Gulf War
- Gramm-Leach-Bliley Act
- September 11th
- Emergency Economic Stabilization Act
- Wall Street Reform Act
- U.S. credit downgrade
- Detroit bankruptcy
- Brexit referendum

Past performance is no guarantee of future results. Hypothetical value of $1 invested at the beginning of 1926. Assumes reinvestment of income and no transaction costs or taxes. This data is for illustrative purposes only and not indicative of any investment. An investment cannot be made directly in an index.

THE LATTE FACTOR CHALLENGE™

DAY _____   DATE _____

	Item: What I bought	Cost: What I spent	Wasted Money? (√ for yes)
1			
2			
3			
4			
5			
6			
7			
8			
9			
10			
11			
12			
13			
14			
15			

My Latte Factor Total: (Total Cost of Checked Items)

$$= \boxed{}$$

THE LATTE FACTOR MATH

My Latte Factor for one day   = _____

My Latte Factor for one month   = _____ (Latte Factor x 30)

My Latte Factor for one year   = _____ (Latte Factor x 365)

My Latte Factor for a decade   = _____ (Latte Factor x 3,650)

IF I INVESTED MY LATTE FACTOR FOR:

10 years it would be worth   = _____

20 years it would be worth   = _____

30 years it would be worth   = _____

40 years it would be worth   = _____

CALCULATING YOUR LATTE FACTOR

To calculate the number above go to www.davidbach.com, click on Latte Factor, and use the Latte Factor calculator.

FREE! MY GIFT TO YOU

To win a free Latte Factor mug, share your Latte Factor experience by emailing us at success@finishrich.com. Just tell us what happened to you when you took the challenge. How much money did you find? What did you learn? Every week a winner will be selected!

THE DOUBLE LATTE FACTOR CHALLENGE

Calculating your Double Latte Factor means looking not just at your daily expenses, but at your weekly, monthly, seasonal, and annual expenses to find items and services big and small that can be eliminated or reduced for big savings.

	Item or Service	Cost	Wasted Money?		Amount Saved	Amount Saved Monthly
	What I bought or buy	How much I spent or spend	✓ if this can be eliminated!	✓ if this can be reduced!	I can save X amount by doing Y!	
Item Example	Bagel with cream cheese and a small coffee	$3.50		✓	$2 per day by eating at home	$60
Service Example	Two cell phones for myself and Alatia	$200/mo. Including all extra fees		✓	$50/mo. by changing service plans	$50
1						
2						
3						
4						
5						
6						
7						
8						
9						
10						
11						
12						
13						
14						
15						
My Double Latte Factor (Total Amount I Can Save Monthly)						$

Acknowledgments

I first want to give a heartfelt thank-you to *you*, my readers. None of what I have done with my life would have been possible without your love, encouragement, and interest in my writings. Over the last year of touring it has been an honor to meet thousands of you at events and hear your personal stories. I am so grateful to you for being here.

My short list of thank-yous on this book includes my agents extraordinaire, Jan Miller and Lacy Lynch. Two decades, ladies, and we're still doing it. Thank you both for believing in me and in this message, and helping me find a home for it. And to Stephen Breimer, my attorney: thank you for two decades of protection, mentorship, and caring. None of what I have done would have been possible without this team.

To John David Mann, my world-class coauthor. Thank you for listening to me talk about this book for over a decade and for believing we would do it when I was finally ready. Working with you on this has truly been a creative pleasure. Here's to many more.

To our publishing team at Atria/Simon & Schuster. To Sarah Pelz, our editor, who connected with this story emotionally and is this book's champion: thank you for caring so much. To Libby McGuire, our publisher, and our entire team at Atria, including Suzanne Donahue, Lindsay Sagnette, Kristin Fassler, Dana Trocker, Lisa Sciambra, Milena Brown, and Melanie Iglesias Pérez: thank you for all you have done and will do to make this book a global sensation.

To Paulo Coelho, who over dinner and drinks in Geneva asked me, "David, what will you write next?" When I told you my dream for *this* book, you smiled and said, "Then, David, you must write your book!" You have no idea how that simple smile and heartfelt look as you said those words have led to these pages. I am forever grateful to you for that evening and for your inspiring book *The Alchemist*.

And finally, to my family. To my grandmother Rose Bach: your inspiration and love led to my entire career and the life I have. I miss you every day. To my parents, Bobbi and Marty Bach, who have always cheered me and constantly asked me, "When are you writing *The Latte Factor*?": thanks for always being there for me; you are truly the greatest parents a kid could ask for. To my wife, Alatia Bradley Bach: the moment I asked you to come start a new life with me and you said "YES" was the luckiest day of my life. You, too, have listened to me talk about this book for ten years, and not once did you question *if* I would do it but only *when*! Thank you for your love. To my two boys, Jack and James: being your father has been the greatest joy of my life. I know this will be a book the two of you will read first. I hope you will always listen to your hearts and your "little boys" and go for your dreams. No regrets, my sons. Your dad loves you now and always!